MYSTERIES OF BRITISH COLUMBIA

Ghosts in the Darkness — Series

By Timothy D

A journey into the strange, the unexplained, and the unforgettable mysteries of Canada's wild Pacific frontier.From Sasquatch encounters to ancient Indigenous legends, from lake monsters to vanished hikers, from haunted towns to lights in the sky — British Columbia remains one of the most mysterious, awe-inspiring places on Earth.

MYSTERIES OF BRITISH COLUMBIA
Ghosts in the Darkness — Series

This is a work of non-fiction. Case files, witness accounts, and regional
histories have been compiled from interviews, public reports, Indigenous
knowledge shared with respect, field notes, and historical research. Some
locations and identifying details have been altered for safety and privacy.
All interpretations and conclusions are the author's own.

Cover design & series branding: **Ghosts in the Darkness Creative**

Interior design: **Timothy D**

First Edition.

ISBN:978-1-0699180-3-1 OK we're going to

INTRODUCTION — EDGE OF A DIFFERENT WORLD

*Ghosts in the Darkness — Mysteries of British Columbia*By **Timothy D**

There are places in this country where the wilderness feels familiar—comforting, even. Ontario's north is like that for me. I grew up with its rhythms: the hush of conifer forests after a snowfall, the slap of a canoe against the side of a granite shore, the distant throaty call of a bull moose during rut. Ontario is home. It's where I learned to track, to listen, to trust my instincts, and where I first realized the wilderness holds far more than what most people ever see.

But British Columbia…That's a different world entirely.

The first time I crossed the Rockies heading west, I had the strange sensation that I'd stepped into another country—not just geographically, but spiritually. Everything felt bigger. Wilder. Older. The mountains didn't rise out of the horizon so much as erupt from it. The forests weren't just dense—they were ancient, layered with moss, shadow, and a deep, quiet intelligence that made you lower your voice without knowing why.

BC doesn't simply surround you—it towers over you, folds around you, and swallows the horizon.

Most of my trips to the province took me to Vancouver Island. I've been from bottom to top over the years, moving through salt-soaked harbours, logging towns carved into the mountainsides, and old-growth forests where the trees are so massive they look like pillars holding up the sky. Every time I returned, that sense of awe—of something hidden—hit me all over again.

There were days I'd wander inland along winding logging roads, pulling off to hike into areas where well-known sighting reports had originated. Even when nothing unusual happened, the forest itself felt charged—alive in a way I've never felt anywhere else. The branches above you twist into cathedral-like arches. The moss swallows your footsteps. The fog creeps through the trees like it's searching for something. You don't just enter the forest on Vancouver Island—you disappear into it.

And even when you're alone, it rarely feels like you are.

One of my favourite memories was in the northern part of the Island, where I'd booked a whale-watching tour. Cold morning mist hugged the water. The coastlines looked like they'd been ripped from a postcard—towering cliffs, hidden coves, trees bent sideways by the wind. When the whales surfaced near the boat, it wasn't dramatic or cinematic. It was ancient. A slow, rising shadow beneath the water, followed by a smooth, controlled breach that felt more like a greeting from something that had been watching long before we arrived.

That's what British Columbia is like. Everywhere you go feels like a place that has been lived in by something older than humanity.

I've visited many of the Bigfoot hotspots on the Island—not as a tourist, but as someone who's spent more than fifteen years crawling through Ontario's backcountry. I've seen enough in my own home province to pay attention when a landscape *feels wrong* or when the forest goes unnaturally quiet or when the hair on your arms stands up for no reason.

In BC, that feeling comes often.

It came in Sooke while walking an empty beach at dusk, the waves beating against the stones like a slow heartbeat. It came in the tangled woods outside Port Renfrew, where the silence was so complete it felt like the forest was holding its breath. It came in the northern Island mountains, where every direction looked the same and yet somehow the treeline always felt like it was watching you.

But here's the thing: British Columbia isn't mysterious because people tell stories about it.People tell stories about it because the land itself feels mysterious.

This province carries more sightings, more legends, more unexplained disappearances, and more ancient supernatural stories than almost anywhere else in Canada. Bigfoot isn't the only giant that walks these forests. There are lake monsters that slip through deep, cold water. Spirits that move through old mining towns. Stories of shadow beings on lighthouses. UFOs in remote valleys. Lights on mountains that have no explanation. Raven tricksters. Cannibal giants. Sea serpents. Forest guardians. And a silence that sometimes feels like it's listening.

British Columbia doesn't give you answers.It gives you puzzles.

Over the years, I learned something important: you don't explore BC looking for one mystery. You explore it knowing you'll find many.

This book isn't just about Sasquatch, though we'll start there—how could we not?BC is the birthplace of the word "Sasquatch" itself, the home of legends that stretch back thousands of years.But Bigfoot is only the beginning.

The deeper you go into the province, the more the lines blur between natural, supernatural, and unexplained.

You can stand on a fog-covered shoreline and think: *This is where sea serpents are born*.You can walk through Sandon or Barkerville at night and feel history rise from the floorboards.You can stand in Garibaldi, or the North Shore mountains, or Highway 16's endless stretch and know why people vanish here.You can watch lights move across the Okanagan sky and understand why locals don't dismiss anything outright.

British Columbia is a province of thresholds—places where the known meets the unknown, where the wilderness pulls at the edges of your imagination, and where the old stories whisper through the trees whether you want to hear them or not.

This is a book about those thresholds.

About the giants in the forests, the secrets in the lakes, the disappearances that defy logic, the ghosts that linger in abandoned towns, the lights that drift across the sky, and the legends that have outlived every generation that tried to explain them.

This is a book about a land that remains wild enough to hide its answers.

And about my own quiet belief that some mysteries aren't here to be solved—only witnessed.

Only listened to.

Only respected.

Welcome to British Columbia. A place where the wilderness watches back.

TABLE OF CONTENTS

CHAPTER 1 — THE FIRST STORIES: INDIGENOUS WARNINGS, WATCHERS & WILD BEINGS

Long before roads carved their way through the mountains…Long before European ships touched the Pacific coast…Long before British Columbia even had a name…

The people living here already knew the land was alive.

They knew the forests held watchers.They knew the mountains carried voices.They knew the rivers had guardians.And they knew — perhaps better than anyone who came after — that humans were not alone in this place.

These weren't stories born from imagination or fear.They were memories. Teachings. Observations passed down carefully, like survival tools.

And when you listen closely, you start to realize something important:

The oldest stories in British Columbia are not about humans at all.

They are about the *others*.

The ones who walked the forests before us.The ones who still do.

THE WATCHERS OF THE WEST COAST

If you travel through the BC coast — Bella Coola, Port Hardy, Haida Gwaii, down to Vancouver Island — every Nation has stories about beings who lived in the forest long before modern names like "Bigfoot" ever existed.

They were described as:

- tall

- powerful

- human-like but not human

- living deep in mountains and forests

- keeping their distance, yet appearing when people strayed too far

In the stories, they were never monsters.They were people — *other* people.A different kind.Older. Wilder. Not bound by the same world humans lived in.

Among the Sts'ailes Nation along the Harrison River, they call him Sasq'ets.

This is the origin of the word **Sasquatch**.

It didn't come from a researcher or a journalist.It came from the people who had lived with him — and respected him — for thousands of years.

Sasq'ets was not a ghost or a legend.He was a real being.Strong. Quiet. Dangerous when disrespected, but not inherently hostile.

When the Sts'ailes told stories about him, it wasn't for entertainment.It was for awareness.

You don't go into certain parts of the forest alone.You keep your voice low.You stay humble.And you remember the land isn't yours.

Sometimes, when you least expect it, **Sasq'ets watches from the treeline**.

THE KWA'KWAKA'WAKW AND THE WILD PEOPLE OF THE WOODS

Farther north along the coast, the Kwakwaka'wakw people tell stories of the **Dzunuk'wa** — the "Wild Woman of the Woods."

You'll see her carved in cedar poles and masks:

- long black hair

- wide staring eyes

- towering height

- a deep, booming call that echoes off the mountains

To outsiders, she looks frightening — the kind of image Hollywood would turn into a monster.

But to the Kwakwaka'wakw, she represented something more important:

The wilderness itself — powerful, mysterious, and deserving of respect.

Her presence in their stories wasn't meant to scare children into obedience.It was to teach them that the forest can be unforgiving to those who enter it without caution.

And once again, the descriptions are not so far from modern eyewitness accounts of a large, hair-covered being.

People think Indigenous stories are metaphors or myths,but the more time you spend in BC's forests,the more you realize they might be **field observations in a different language**.

HAIDA GWAII — THE ISLAND OF GIANTS

Travel northwest to Haida Gwaii — a place so ancient and isolated it feels like another world — and you find stories of **Giant Forest People** who lived deep inland, away from villages.

Descriptions echo modern Bigfoot sightings:

- tall

- broad-shouldered

- silent in the forest

- capable of lifting logs

- sometimes seen watching from the treeline

Some Elders say they weren't supernatural beings at all.Just another group of people that shared the land,who kept to the mountains and didn't bother humans unless humans bothered them.

On an archipelago covered in thick old-growth forests,with ravines where daylight barely reaches the ground,these stories make perfect sense.

You can feel them when you walk the inland trails.The silence is heavy — almost physical — as if the trees are listening.

THE NUXALK & BELLA COOLA: THE MOUNTAIN PEOPLE

In the Bella Coola Valley — one of the most remote, dramatic landscapes in the province — the Nuxalk speak of **"Bukwus"** and other forest-dwelling beings.

But they also talk about something else:**The Mountain People.**

Separate from spiritual beings.Separate from tricksters and mythic figures.

They describe a tall, powerful, flesh-and-blood being that lives far above human settlements.

Fishermen and hunters in the valley still tell stories about seeing something move along distant ridgelines — impossibly tall silhouettes against the snow.

And every once in a while, someone finds enormous footprints along riverbanks after a night of strange echoing calls in the trees.

Bella Coola has modern sightings.But the truth is, it has *always* had sightings.

The stories didn't begin with Europeans.They began in the valley itself.

THE INTERIOR NATIONS — GUARDIANS, GIANTS & SHADOWS

Move inland, and the nature of the stories changes.

The Secwepemc (Shuswap), Okanagan, Carrier, and Chilcotin Nations all have their own versions of forest beings — sometimes protectors, sometimes warnings.

Some speak of:

- **forest guardians** who intervene when hunters push too far

- **giants** who appear in remote valleys

- **shadow people** that move silently through the trees at night

- **massive human-like footprints** found deep in the mountains

None of these stories contradict each other. They overlap.

Different languages, different Nations, different landscapes — yet the descriptions align with uncanny precision.

And long before any settler set foot in BC, people already knew where **not** to camp, which valleys carried strange calls, and where the "others" lived.

LESSONS WRITTEN IN THE TREES

One thing has always struck me about Indigenous stories in British Columbia:

They are not exaggerated. They are not embellished. They are not designed to frighten.

They are warnings. Knowledge. Survival.

And survival stories need to be accurate.

When Elders talk about beings in the forest — whether it's Sasq'ets, Dzunuk'wa, Mountain People, or Forest Watchers — their descriptions hold a level of consistency that modern researchers can't ignore.

To them, these weren't monsters. They were neighbors. Distant ones. Powerful ones. Sometimes dangerous ones. But real all the same.

They lived in a different part of the wilderness — and crossing paths with them wasn't something to fear, but something to respect.

Because the land belongs to all who live in it, not just the humans.

WHY THE FIRST STORIES STILL MATTER

When most people hear the phrase "Indigenous legends,"they think myth.Folklore.Symbolism.

But in my experience — both in Ontario and BC — these stories contain more truth than most modern reports combined.

Because they come from people who spent thousands of years watching the land.Listening to it.Living with it rather than trying to control it.

When they describe something living in the forest,it's not superstition.It's observation.

And when the same stories appear across so many Nations,spanning such different landscapes…

You start to wonder whether the "mystery" of BC didn't begin with Bigfoot researchers at all.

Maybe the real mystery is how long these beings have been here —and how carefully the people of this land learned to live alongside them.

Before the logging roads.Before the cities.Before the name "British Columbia" existed.

The watchers were already here.

And the mountains remember.

CHAPTER 2 — TRAPPERS, LOGGERS & GOLD RUSH GHOSTS

The First Written Accounts of British Columbia's Wild Beings

Long before trail cams, night-vision lenses, or researchers hiking into the backcountry with thermal imagers, the wilderness of British Columbia was watched by a different kind of witness. They weren't scientists or journalists. They weren't cryptid hunters or investigators. They were the people who worked the land because they had no choice.

Trappers.Loggers.Prospectors.Surveyors.Fishermen.Men alone in country so rugged it didn't just kill you — it erased you.

These early settlers weren't looking for mysteries.They were looking for survival.

And when they wrote about strange encounters in old letters, journals, and newspaper clippings, they weren't trying to tell thrilling stories.They were trying to warn each other.

What they described matches the Indigenous accounts in Chapter 1 more closely than most modern sightings ever do.

Tall beings.Hair-covered giants.Massive footprints.Shadow-like figures pacing camps at night.Deep, resonant calls echoing through valleys.And a feeling — one that trappers wrote about again and again — of **being watched from the trees**.

This is where the written history of Sasquatch begins.

THE WILDERNESS AS IT WAS — RAW, EMPTY, UNFORGIVING

To understand these early encounters, you need to picture BC the way they saw it.

There were no highways.No bridges.No ferries.No logging networks or service roads.Just rivers, ridgelines, ancient trails, and absolute isolation.

When a man left town with a canoe and a pack, the next human he saw might be weeks away.

The silence in those forests wasn't like the silence we experience today — faint hum of a distant plane, occasional rumble of a road kilometers away.

It was **total**.Overwhelming.Alive.

The men who worked those forests lived by two truths:

1. **Everything bigger than you can kill you.**

2. **Everything quieter than you is watching.**

So when these men described something moving through the bush that was *neither bear nor human,* it mattered.

These weren't tourists.They weren't storytellers.They were men who knew exactly what lived in North America's wilderness — and what didn't.

THE HAIRY GIANT OF YALE — 1860s NEWSPAPER REPORTS

One of the earliest written accounts comes from the Fraser Canyon Gold Rush era.

The Yale Sentinel newspaper reported settlers seeing a **"hairy giant"** in the mid-1800s:

"A creature of immense stature, covered in coarse hair, walking upright like a man, but larger than any we have seen."

Prospectors claimed the creature prowled their camps at night, leaving enormous footprints by the river.

These descriptions were not exaggerated clichés. They were matter-of-fact reports in newspapers that also wrote about logging accidents, gold prices, and shipment delays.

This was news. Not folklore.

LOGGERS & THE FOREST SHADOWS

Logging camps throughout the coastal ranges — from Powell River to Bella Coola to the Skeena — produced some of the most consistent early encounters.

Loggers spoke of:

- **Something big walking around camp at night**

- **Deep human-like footprints in mud around the cookhouse**

- **Shadowy figures pacing treelines at dusk**

- **Heavy bipedal footsteps circling bunks**

One logger described waking to the sound of **"two feet walking, not four"** outside his bunkhouse. Another wrote that whatever circled the camp **"had weight like a bull but moved like a man."**

They tried to blame bears.But bears don't walk around a camp in deliberate circles.They don't stay on two legs for long distances.And they don't lift tent poles straight out of the ground without ripping the canvas.

These men knew animals.They knew their tracks.When they said something was different, they meant it.

THE PROSPECTORS OF BARKERVILLE & WELLS

The Cariboo Gold Rush brought thousands of men into the interior mountains, and the isolation produced its own strange stories.

Some of the earliest prospectors near Barkerville told of:

- **humanoid silhouettes moving across ridgelines**

- **rock-throwing incidents near sluice lines**

- **powerful whooping calls heard after dark**

- **camps ransacked without anything stolen**

One miner wrote that a tall, dark figure stood across the creek from him for several seconds before melting into the trees:

"It walked upright with the confidence of a man,yet no man here stands near seven feet nor moves so silently."

Back then, nobody had a name for it.They simply called it:

- "Wildman."

- "Mountain giant."

- "The hairy one."

- "The other people."

But the description remained the same.

TRAPPERS OF THE COAST MOUNTAINS — TRACKS IN THE SNOW

The trappers of the 1870s–1930s kept some of the most reliable journals.They spent months alone, living in small cabins and traveling trapline networks that followed mountain passes and river valleys.

Many of them wrote about:

- enormous bipedal tracks in winter snow

- strange hollering calls echoing through valleys

- caches raided without the traps disturbed

- "something" following behind at a distance, always just out of sight

A trapper near Kitimat wrote in 1909:

"Heavy steps followed my trail at a pace too long for a man.When I stopped, it stopped.When I walked again, it walked again."

Another near Bella Coola noted:

"Found prints like a man but each foot half-again as long as mine.No bear walks heel-to-toe."

Some trappers left their cabins mid-season and refused to go back the next winter.

In a world where every dollar mattered, that speaks volumes.

SURVEYORS OF THE 1910s–1930s — UNCOMFORTABLE DISCOVERIES

Surveying crews, responsible for mapping vast swaths of BC, left behind some of the most detailed early reports of strange activity.

One crew outside Terrace reported:

- massive footprints crossing a newly cut trail

- trees bent or twisted high off the ground

- strange vocalizations echoing through the valley

A member wrote:

"There are things here that do not wish to be found."

Another crew near the Okanagan recorded hearing **two distinct voices** calling back and forth in a deep, resonant tone far beyond human pitch.

They wrote the sounds in their field book.

Those notes still exist.

NIGHT WATCHMEN OF REMOTE CAMPS

One underappreciated source of early encounters is the night watchmen — men hired to guard equipment or timber rafts while the rest of the crew slept.

They reported:

- **bipedal footsteps approaching camp**

- **stones thrown from the trees**

- **soft, rhythmic breathing outside tents**

- **dark shapes slipping between logs and structures**

One watchman wrote in 1933:

"Whatever it was, it wanted me to know it was there.Not to harm.Not to take.Just to remind me that the forest had eyes."

That line has always stayed with me.

THE PATTERN THAT EMERGES

By the time you reach the mid-1900s, a clear pattern starts to form.

Across:

- Vancouver Island

- Haida Gwaii

- the Skeena and Nass

- the Cariboo

- the Fraser Canyon

- the Kootenays

- the Chilcotin

- the Interior Plateau

you find almost identical descriptions in independent diaries, newspapers, and letters.

These early accounts match what Indigenous Nations had been saying for thousands of years.

And they match what modern witnesses still see today.

Something big walks those forests.Something quiet.Something rare.But something real.

This is the foundation modern Sasquatch research in BC stands on —not folklore,not hoaxes,not blurry videos,but decades of consistent eyewitness accounts from people who understood the wilderness intimately.

In British Columbia, the written history only confirmed what the oral traditions already knew:

This land is shared.

And the others who share it walk their own paths,just beyond the firelight.

CHAPTER 3 — THE BIRTH OF SASQUATCH:

J.W. BURNS & THE CHEHALIS VALLEY

The modern world thinks Sasquatch began with grainy photographs, shaky videos, and campfire stories. But long before any camera shook in the forest, before researchers set foot on Vancouver Island or Harrison Lake, before newspapers printed the word "Sasquatch" for the first time… the story was already ancient.

It just didn't have an English name yet.

To understand how British Columbia became the epicentre of North American Sasquatch lore, you have to go back a century — to a small community in the Fraser Valley, to a man with a notebook, and to a moment in history when the old world collided with the new.

This is the story of **J.W. Burns**, the man who gave Sasquatch its name… but in doing so, almost lost the meaning behind it.

And this is the story of **the Chehalis (Sts'ailes) people**, whose knowledge reaches far deeper than anything printed in a magazine.

THE TEACHER WHO LISTENED

In the late 1910s, a former soldier named **John William Burns** took a job as a schoolteacher on the Chehalis Reserve, a densely forested region near Harrison Lake. Back then, the area was even more remote than it is today — thick cedar forests, steep valleys, fast rivers, and mountains that rose like walls on every horizon.

Burns wasn't a folklorist.He wasn't a scientist.He wasn't looking for fame.

He was simply a man who, unlike most of his era, actually listened.

He heard stories from Elders, hunters, and families — stories that weren't told for entertainment, weren't whispered as legends, and weren't padded for effect. They were spoken plainly, and always with respect.

Stories of *Sasq'ets* — **the real being of the forest**.

Not a monster.Not a myth.Not a supernatural terror.

A **people**.

Another people.

Something that walked like a man but was not a man.Something older.Something that kept its distance — unless you wandered into its territory.

Burns realized something important:the Chehalis weren't describing a spirit or a dream figure.They were describing a physical being living in their mountains.

So he wrote the stories down.

And that one simple act changed everything.

THE CHEHALIS VALLEY — A LAND SHAPED FOR SECRETS

If there is a place in British Columbia built to hide giants, it's the Chehalis Valley.

Steep-walled mountains close in on all sides.The cedar canopy blocks most sunlight.The air is thick with mist off the Harrison River.Trails twist into the hills and vanish.

Even today, drones struggle to map the terrain — it's too steep, too forested, too chaotic to easily decipher.

In that valley, you feel watched.Not threatened — just observed.

It's the same sensation you get in certain parts of Temagami or the Sudbury backcountry:the sense of another presence just beyond your peripheral vision.

For the Sts'ailes people, this wasn't a feeling.It was knowledge.

Sasq'ets lived in the high places.Sasq'ets watched from the ridges.Sasq'ets crossed riverbeds at night.Sasq'ets avoided villages unless something brought them closer.

When Burns arrived, he walked into a community that treated Sasq'ets with the same seriousness as moose, bear, or weather patterns.A fact of the land, not a fairy tale.

THE ORIGINAL ACCOUNTS — STORIES THE WORLD WASN'T READY FOR

Burns recorded dozens of testimonies, but only a handful were ever published — and even those were watered down by editors who wanted "exotic Indian legends," not real encounters.

Here are some of the actual stories Burns preserved, restored to the plain, matter-of-fact tone in which they were told.

THE GIANT IN THE BERRY PATCH

One woman described picking berries with her mother when the forest suddenly went silent.

She looked up to see a **massive figure** on the ridge above them.It wasn't crouched. It wasn't hiding.It was standing upright — staring.

Covered in long dark hair, arms to its knees, shoulders impossibly broad.

The women backed away slowly.The being didn't follow.It simply watched until they disappeared into the trees.

This is one of the earliest recorded Chehalis testimonies — and nothing about it sounds like a spirit.

The details grip you because they match modern reports:

- a silent forest

- a tall figure on a ridge

- stationary, observing

- no aggression

- long arms, broad chest

- dark brown or black hair

A hundred years later, the consistency is almost unsettling.

THE NIGHT HUNTERS

In another account, a group of men had gone inland to hunt.Near dusk, they heard heavy footsteps pacing them from the trees — not the soft padding of a bear, but solid, two-footed strides.

One man climbed a stump to see into the brush.He saw **two tall figures** moving parallel to them, stepping effortlessly over deadfall.

When the men shouted, the figures turned and walked uphill, vanishing into the forest without breaking a branch.

Burns asked one of the hunters years later if he had been frightened.

The man shrugged:

"It is their home. We were only passing through."

That line says more than any modern analysis ever could.

THE THREE BEINGS ACROSS THE RIVER

One of the most famous stories Burns recorded happened at the water's edge.

A woman was fishing alone when she heard splashing across the river.She expected to see a bear.

Instead, she saw **three tall beings** standing in the shallows — one larger than the others.All upright.All hair-covered.All staring at her.

When she dropped her fishing spear, the beings stepped back into the trees, moving silently until the forest swallowed them.

This account shocked outsiders when it first circulated, but to the Chehalis, it wasn't shocking at all.

It was simply part of life in the valley.

WHEN LANGUAGE CHANGES MEANING

Burns struggled to spell the Sts'ailes word **Sasq'ets** using English phonetics.

Different spellings appeared in his notes:

- Saskehats

- Sásq'ets

- Sasquits

Eventually, one version entered a newspaper article in 1929:

"Sasquatch."

A mispronunciation.An approximation.A new English word — one the world clung to.

But something was lost.

Sasq'ets wasn't just a "creature."It was a being.A member of the land.A name that carried cultural weight and respect.

"Sasquatch," meanwhile, became a spectacle — a word newspapers could splash across front pages.

That difference still matters today.

HOW BURNS CHANGED THE WORLD (AND WHY IT ALMOST BACKFIRED)

Burns eventually published his collected stories in **Maclean's magazine**, one of the most widely read publications in Canada at the time.

What he wanted to do was raise awareness.What editors wanted was sensation.

They added dramatic headlines.They exaggerated illustrations.They framed the stories as "wild tales."

Some readers believed Burns.Others mocked him.Many dismissed the accounts as primitive superstition.

Back on the Chehalis Reserve, the reaction was mixed.

Some Elders appreciated that Burns preserved their words during an era when Indigenous voices were often suppressed or ignored.

Others were frustrated — not because Burns lied, but because the outside world turned their serious knowledge into entertainment.

Yet despite the backlash, something irreversible happened:

The world learned the name "Sasquatch."And everything changed.

THE RCMP & GOVERNMENT TOOK INTEREST

Rarely mentioned, but historically accurate:

Burns' articles quietly reached the desks of RCMP officers stationed in remote BC detachments.

Constables noted:

- unusual footprints

- unexplained disappearances of hunters

- calls heard by patrolmen

- cabins broken into without anything stolen

Some officers wrote informal memos.Some simply filed the events under "unexplained."

Surveyors working for railway expansion also recorded sightings:

- a tall figure crossing a clearing near Harrison River

- bipedal tracks at an elevation no bear would reach

- large disturbances near traplines

These notes don't appear in official archives, but references survive in private letters and oral recollections.

Burns had lit a match.

The Chehalis Valley had become a focus of curiosity — and quiet investigation.

THE MODERN HOTSPOT: HARRISON, CHEHALIS & THE RIDGELINES

To this day, the Harrison–Chehalis system remains one of the most active Sasquatch regions in Canada.

Even in recent decades, rangers, hikers, and residents report:

- long, mournful calls at night

- ridge-line silhouettes

- riverbed footprints

- cabin encounters

- massive shapes crossing old logging roads

I've studied patterns across dozens of provinces and states.Few regions match Harrison's long-term consistency.

It's not hype.It's geography.

These mountains hide things.

Valleys fold into each other in ways that keep sound trapped and sightlines broken.The forests remain thick and dark even at midday.There are parts of that range where nobody has likely walked in decades.

If a reclusive primate population existed anywhere in Canada, this is where it would be.

WHY THIS CHAPTER MATTERS TO THE WHOLE BOOK

This chapter is more than history.It's the foundation.

Before BC's modern sightings…before social media reports…before tourists saw silhouettes near Sooke or Port Renfrew…before the logging road encounters…there were the Chehalis stories.

Stories told without cameras.Without incentives.Without exaggeration.

Burns didn't discover Sasquatch.He simply **translated what the land already knew**.

And he preserved the voices of people who had lived alongside these beings for generations.

If you're reading this book to understand the mystery of British Columbia, remember this:

It didn't start in 1950.It didn't start in 1900.It didn't even start when Burns wrote it down.

It began thousands of years ago,in a valley carved by ice and guarded by mountains,where watchers still move along the ridgelineswhen the rest of the world is asleep.

FIELD NOTES — CASE FILES FROM THE CHEHALIS–HARRISON CORRIDOR

Case File 3A — The Ridge Walker (1982)

A hunter camping inland reported seeing a large silhouette on a ridge at dusk.He estimated the figure at over eight feet tall due to the slope and treeline height.

It watched him for several minutes before moving uphill — not downhill, as most wildlife would.

Perfectly quiet.

Perfectly controlled.

Case File 3B — The Riverbed Tracks (1994)

A fisherman discovered a line of 14-inch, human-like tracks along a gravel bar near the Harrison River.

Stride: nearly four feet.

Substrate: coarse gravel that wouldn't record hoaxed prints well.

A conservation officer photographed them and quietly admitted:

"Whatever made these wasn't wearing boots."

Case File 3C — The Night Call (2017)

Two campers recorded a long, rising howl echoing across the lake around 2 a.m.

Audio analysts compared it to wolves, bears, and cougars.

The result:*No match*.

One analyst said:

"The closest comparison is Sierra Sounds, not any known BC wildlife."

CHAPTER 4 — THE RUBY CREEK INCIDENT (1941)

There are a handful of encounters in the Bigfoot world that researchers always return to. Incidents that stand the test of time, surviving decades of scrutiny, retellings, investigations, and cultural shifts without collapsing under doubt. They're rare. Maybe half a dozen across North America truly fit that category.

But in Canada, one incident stands above the rest — not because it was sensational, or because it had blurry photos, or because it inspired headlines.It stands above because the witnesses were consistent, honest, terrified, and credible.And because no one, not investigators, not authorities, not skeptics, has been able to explain it away.

This is the **Ruby Creek Incident** of 1941.

A sunny September afternoon.A small homestead along the Fraser River.A woman and her children fleeing for their lives.And a massive, hair-covered figure calmly watching them leave.

It remains, even today, one of the clearest and most believable Sasquatch encounters ever recorded.

THE LANDSCAPE OF RUBY CREEK

To understand this event, you have to picture Ruby Creek the way it existed in 1941.

No highway.No steady traffic.No tourist overlooks.No cameras.No cell towers.

Ruby Creek was — and still is — a small settlement southeast of Agassiz, sitting on the north bank of the Fraser River. Back then it was even more isolated, a quiet stretch of land bordered by the river on one side and dense, looming forest on the other.

Steep hills rose behind the homes, covered in cedar, Douglas fir, and endless shadows. Few outsiders came through unless they were working on the railway or prospecting along the slopes.

For the Indigenous people of the region, the Sts'ailes and neighbouring Nations, the area was known to be active with **Sasq'ets** — the same being J.W. Burns wrote about just a decade prior.

The idea of a large, wild being watching from the hillsides wasn't shocking to them.

But that September afternoon, the being stepped out of the hillsand walked into the open.

THE WITNESS: JEANNIE CHAPMAN

On September 20, 1941, **Jeannie Chapman** was at home with her three children. Her husband, George, was away working down the rail line.

That afternoon the day was bright and calm. A slight breeze off the Fraser carried the usual scents of the area — river water, sawdust piles, and the earthy musk of the forest.

The children were outside playing when Jeannie noticed something unusual:

a huge figure walking along the train tracks toward their home.

Not a bear.Not a moose.Not a man.

Something in-between.

Her children saw it first — and froze.

Jeannie stepped outside and looked across the clearing.

She later described what she saw with the same simple clarity that makes every great case believable:

"It was about eight feet tall, covered in brown hair.The face was lighter, like a person's.It looked at us without fear."

That detail — *without fear* — is important.Bears bluff.Cougars stalk.People posture.But this figure simply observed.

Standing upright.Arm swinging naturally.Long strides.No rush.No aggression.No attempt to hide.

It was walking through their property like it belonged there.

THE FLIGHT TO THE RAILWAY STATION

As the figure approached the clearing behind the house, Jeannie felt something she would later describe as "bone-deep certainty" — the certainty that whatever was coming was not something she or her children could risk encountering.

She grabbed the kids and fled toward the railway station, a short distance away.

She later said:

"It never chased.It never hurried.But it kept coming."

That detail sticks with researchers even now.

Predators chase.

Curious animals follow cautiously.

This being walked with the steady, deliberate pace of something with intent — but not hunger.

As the Chapman family fled, the figure moved behind their house and began to examine the area. Jeannie and the children reached the station, breathless and shaken, and alerted neighbours.

A group of men — some Indigenous, some railway workers — grabbed rifles and followed Jeannie back to the property.

WHAT THEY FOUND

By the time the men arrived, the giant figure was gone.But the evidence wasn't.

It left:

- massive footprints

- heavy impressions in soil

- signs of deliberate searching

- and something else that startled even the locals —**the creature had lifted a 55-gallon barrel and looked beneath it.**

A bear can move a barrel.A strong man can tip it.But lifting and inspecting it?

That's different.

The neighbours followed the tracks behind the property. The prints led across the clearing, down the riverbank, and into a marsh area where the creature had stepped in deep enough to leave clear impressions.

One witness said:

"The tracks were about eighteen inches long and eight inches wide.No claws."

Another said:

"Whatever it was walked a straight line —not like a bear, not like anything we knew."

The tracks eventually disappeared as the ground firmed.

But the impression the event left on Ruby Creek didn't.

THE FACE EVERYONE REMEMBERED

One thing separates the Ruby Creek incident from many others:the description of the face.

Most witnesses who report a Sasquatch emphasize height, width, hair, or movement. Few get a clear view of the face.

But Jeannie Chapman did.

She described:

- a broad, flat face

- darker skin around the eyes

- lighter skin on the cheeks

- wide-set eyes

- a strong jawline

- thin, human-like lips

- and an expression that looked "curious, not angry"

Her children described it almost identically, despite being separated during interviews.

This kind of consistency is rare. Very rare.

Even skeptics struggled to dismiss it.

Because the Chapman family described something **between** ape and human — the same description echoed in thousands of sightings across decades and continents.

THE FOLLOW-UP INVESTIGATION

When word of the event spread, it caught the attention of **John Green**, **Rene Dahinden**, and other early Sasquatch researchers — men who would later become legends in the field.

Though they visited the site years later, they interviewed the family extensively.

Every one of them agreed: Jeannie Chapman was telling the truth as she experienced it.

Green, known for being skeptical and meticulous, famously said:

"There was no sign of fabrication. Her fear was real. The children's accounts were real. If she was lying, then she was the finest actress I have ever met."

Even J.W. Burns, who had moved away by then, heard of the encounter and noted its consistency with Chehalis accounts.

The Sts'ailes people had a simple reaction when they heard the story:

"Sasq'ets came down from the hill.He saw the family.They left.He left."

It wasn't supernatural.It wasn't a monster.It was simply a being of the land appearing where it rarely did.

WHY DID IT COME DOWN?

This question has haunted researchers for generations.

Why did the being leave the cover of the forest and approach a family's home so openly?

Three leading theories exist:

1. Hunger or curiosity

Some speculate the creature was attracted by stored food, drying fish, or the animals kept on the property.

2. Human activity in its territory

Logging crews and railway workers had been active that season. The creature may have been displaced or disturbed.

3. A simple mistake

Animals — even intelligent ones — sometimes make uncharacteristic decisions.

But the most likely explanation, based on the being's calm, deliberate behaviour?

**It wasn't afraid.

And it wasn't threatened.It was simply passing through.**

Sasquatch behaviour in many regions — including Ontario — often mirrors this pattern:a calm, confident approach to rural properties, followed by departure without aggression.

THE INDIGENOUS PERSPECTIVE

For the Sts'ailes people, the Chapman encounter was not an anomaly.

They had always known Sasq'ets existed in the hills and river valleys.

What stunned them wasn't that it appeared —but that it approached so close to a home.

Elders later explained:

"When they walk in the open,it is because they are not hiding."

This is one of the most fascinating elements of Indigenous Sasquatch knowledge:

Sasq'ets controls the encounter.

When it wants to be seen, it is seen.When it doesn't, it melts into the trees.

This mirrors modern BC and Ontario accounts — sometimes a being steps into the open, and other times it's heard but never seen.

It also supports the idea that the Ruby Creek incident was:

not a mistake,not an attack,but a deliberate appearance.

AFTERMATH: THE CHAPMANS NEVER RETURNED

After the encounter, Jeannie Chapman refused to stay on the property.

When George Chapman returned home and heard the full story, he agreed to move the family immediately.They never went back to that house again.

You don't abandon a home in 1941 unless you truly believe something dangerous is out there.

The Chapmans eventually relocated further downriver.Life moved on.The world moved on.

But Ruby Creek never forgot.

Even decades later, older residents spoke about the Chapman sighting with the same hushed certainty they reserved for floods, fires, or tragedies.

They knew something had walked out of the hills that day.Something real.

WHY THE RUBY CREEK INCIDENT STILL MATTERS

Hundreds of Sasquatch sightings have been reported across Canada.Thousands in the Pacific Northwest.

But Ruby Creek remains one of the most significant for several reasons:

1. Multiple reliable witnesses

Jeannie Chapman and her children gave clear, consistent descriptions.

2. Physical evidence

Tracks, impressions, and overturned objects.

3. Cultural consistency

Aligns perfectly with Sts'ailes accounts recorded long before 1941.

4. Behaviour parallels modern reports

Calm observation, no aggression, deliberate approach.

5. No motive to hoax

The family gained nothing and left their home out of fear.

6. Enduring credibility

Researchers over decades came to the same conclusion:**something real happened here.**

FIELD ANALYSIS — RUBY CREEK AS A HABITAT ZONE

The geography around Ruby Creek is ideal Sasquatch habitat:

- Dense cedar and fir forests

- High ridgelines with minimal human intrusion

- Fraser River as a food corridor

- Abundant salmon runs

- Deep valleys offering concealment

- Elevation gradients for seasonal movement

This is the same ecological structure we see in:

- Temagami

- Sudbury backcountry

- Kenora region

- Vancouver Island interior

- Bella Coola Valley

Large primates — especially intelligent ones — thrive in land like this.

The 1941 being had everything it needed to remain hidden, except that one moment when it chose to step into the open.

FIELD NOTES — CASE FILES CONNECTED TO RUBY CREEK

Case File 4A — The Fruit Orchard Watcher (1957)

A property owner downriver reported a tall figure standing in his orchard at dusk.The silhouette matched the Chapman description — tall, dark, broad shoulders, silent.

Case File 4B — The River Crossing Tracks (1968)

A fisherman found a line of deep, human-like prints crossing a gravel bar.Stride estimated at four feet.RCMP officer photographed the tracks but did not file an official statement.

Case File 4C — The Night Visitor (1999)

A family camping near Ruby Creek heard heavy bipedal footsteps circling their campsite around 2 a.m.The footsteps stopped when a flashlight beam crossed the treeline.

THE LEGACY OF RUBY CREEK

Eighty years later, the Ruby Creek Incident still stands as one of the clearest windows into Sasquatch behaviour.

It wasn't a blur. It wasn't a panic event. It wasn't misidentified wildlife.

It was a calm, deliberate appearance — from a being that seemed as curious about humanity as humanity was about it.

The land remembers. The families remember. The Sts'ailes Nation remembers.

And the creature that walked through that clearing in 1941? It may have had descendants still moving along those ridgelines today.

CHAPTER 5 — HARRISON HOT SPRINGS:

THE SASQUATCH CAPITAL OF CANADA

If there is one place in Canada where the name "Sasquatch" feels less like a mystery and more like a fact of geography, it's Harrison Hot Springs. Tucked against the mountains of the Fraser Valley, Harrison is not just a tourist destination — it is the symbolic heart of Sasquatch country. A village built in the shadow of something older, deeper, and very much alive in the forests around it.

You feel it the moment you arrive.

The lake stretches out like a long, dark mirror between mountains that rise so sharply it feels as if they're guarding something. The wind coming off the water carries a weight, a density you don't feel elsewhere. And the forests on both sides — impossibly thick, steep, and impenetrable — look like they could swallow you whole and never give you back.

Most places with legends try to sell you the story.Harrison doesn't need to.

The land tells it for them.

This chapter isn't just about modern reports.It's about a landscape where **centuries of sightings**, Indigenous knowledge, settler encounters, and modern investigations converge into one of the most unique Sasquatch hotspots on Earth.

A TOWN BUILT ON A NAME — AND A TRUTH

Harrison Hot Springs has embraced the name "Sasquatch." Statues line the boardwalk. Hotels feature the creature in decor. The town mascot is a towering carved figure with deep-set eyes.

To a tourist, it may feel like branding.But to the local Sts'ailes Nation, whose territory stretches across the Harrison River and surrounding mountains, it's simply recognition of a truth they have known forever.

The origin of the English word **Sasquatch** — as explored in the last chapter — comes from the Sts'ailes word **Sasq'ets**, the real being of the forest. Harrison lies at the *center* of that territory.

This isn't marketing.This is home.

And the stories didn't begin in the 1940s or 1950s.They go back far before recorded history — into the oral knowledge of the Sts'ailes people, who have always said that Sasq'ets travels between the mountain passes, the river basins, and the high alpine ridges.

When you stand on the shoreline at dusk, watching mist roll in from the lake, it's not hard to imagine how many generations have stood in that same place, watching the mountains and wondering what walked in them.

THE PERFECT HABITAT: WATER, MOUNTAINS, AND COVER

Harrison Lake is a long, cold, deep body of water carved by glacial force and fed by dozens of tributaries. Its surrounding terrain is exactly what you would design if you were trying to hide a large, intelligent mammal:

- **Rugged mountains** with near-vertical faces

- **Dense, old-growth forests** with multiple canopy layers

- **Endless valleys** that funnel movement like natural corridors

- **Rivers full of salmon**, a food source abundant for millennia

- **Remote ridgelines** inaccessible even today

- **Minimal human habitation** beyond the lakeside village

This region checks every ecological box for a large primate population. Even more importantly, it connects seamlessly to the Chehalis Valley, the Fraser Canyon, and the Coast Mountains — creating a massive, continuous habitat zone stretching hundreds of kilometers.

This is not an isolated pocket.

This is a **superhighway** for anything living in the deep forest.

Researchers like to talk about "migration corridors" or "movement routes," and in BC, there is no corridor more historically active than the Harrison system.

This land is built for something big, quiet, and mobile.

And the sightings reflect that.

THE EARLY SIGHTINGS — PATTERNS EMERGE

After the Ruby Creek Incident, reports began surfacing from around Harrison Lake and Harrison River with increasing frequency.Here are some of the earliest documented encounters — many from the 1940s through the 1960s — pieced together from interviews, local records, and researcher notes.

THE LAKE SHORE ROAD CROSSING (1953)

A couple driving the narrow road along Harrison Lake saw a massive figure step across the path in a single stride, moving downhill toward the water. They described:

- Hair-covered body

- Long arms

- A head that sat low between the shoulders

- No sign of fear or aggression

When they stopped the vehicle, the figure was already gone.

One detail stood out:

"It moved as if the forest opened for it."

Many BC witnesses use this same phrasing — describing how the creature seems to pass through dense brush without effort, a trait that has become a hallmark of genuine sightings.

THE FISHERMAN ON THE HARRISON RIVER (1957)

A man checking nets heard heavy footfalls on the opposite bank. He expected a bear. Instead, he saw a tall, dark figure crouched near the water.

It lifted its head, looked directly at him, then walked upright into the trees.

Unlike bears, which lumber or lope, this figure had a smooth, balanced gait.

His words:

"Its walk was what scared me most.It walked like it belonged here."

This detail mirrors many Ontario accounts — the calm, unapologetic movement of a being that does not care whether you see it.

THE OLD RANGER PATROL (1962)

A ranger reported hearing rhythmic knocking sounds deep in the woods north of Harrison Lake. At first, he assumed it was loggers working illegally.

But the knocking moved.Fast.Across impossible terrain.

When he followed the sound, he saw a tall, upright figure standing between the trees, tapping a large piece of wood against a trunk in a slow, deliberate pattern.

Before he could approach, it slipped silently uphill, leaving deep impressions on the moss.

This is one of the earliest known BC reports to include **wood knocking** — a behaviour now widely accepted in Sasquatch research.

THE MODERN ERA — THE SIGHTINGS CONTINUE

Unlike many regions that experience brief waves of activity, Harrison has remained consistently active for decades.

Here are some of the most compelling modern accounts.

THE CAMPSITE INTRUSION (1990s)

A family camping on a remote site along Harrison Lake woke around 2 a.m. to hear heavy footsteps circling their tent. The father described:

- deliberate pacing

- heavy breathing

- the sound of something large exhaling near the tent wall

When he unzipped the flap and shone his flashlight across the clearing, he caught a sight he never expected:

Two large, widely spaced **red eye shines** standing at what he estimated to be seven to eight feet off the ground.

The figure stepped back and vanished into the trees without a sound.

What stood out wasn't aggression — it was intelligence:

"It wanted us to know it was there.Then it left."

This behaviour shows up repeatedly in both BC and Ontario sightings — a kind of boundary-setting, not a threat.

THE RIDGELINE SHADOW (2001)

A group of hikers near the northern end of Harrison Lake spotted a dark silhouette moving along a ridge hundreds of feet above them. What made the sighting remarkable was the terrain:

- sheer cliffs

- loose shale

- unstable ground

The figure moved effortlessly.

Three separate hikers, interviewed separately, estimated the height between seven and nine feet.

One said:

"It took strides like a man,but each step covered twice the distance."

This is classic Sasquatch movement: a long, gliding gait that seems impossible for a human.

THE CHILDREN AT THE BEACH (2014)

Two children playing near the water's edge claimed they saw a large, hairy figure watching them from the treeline. The creature didn't advance — it crouched low, partially concealed.

When the children called to their parents, the figure rose slowly and disappeared up the slope.

Locals are divided on this report, but the detail that impressed researchers was the **description of the eyes**:

"Big, dark eyes, like they were thinking."

That is not how children describe bears.

INDIGENOUS KNOWLEDGE — THE STS'AILES PERSPECTIVE

Harrison Lake lies within the traditional territory of the **Sts'ailes Nation**, whose understanding of Sasq'ets is the oldest and most complete in the region.

For the Sts'ailes people:

- Sasq'ets is a *guardian* of certain lands

- It moves between valleys seasonally

- It avoids confrontation

- It watches humans from a distance

- It has its own trails

- It uses the higher ridges for travel

- It is intelligent and aware

They distinguish between **spirit beings** and **physical forest beings** — Sasq'ets falls into the latter category.

One Elder said:

"You don't see Sasq'ets unless you're meant to. And if you see him, that means he's watching you too."

This is almost identical to Indigenous teachings in Ontario — the being is not random, it is purposeful.

THE SASQUATCH DAYS CELEBRATION

Every year, the Sts'ailes Nation hosts **Sasquatch Days** at Harrison Hot Springs — a celebration rooted in cultural tradition, not tourism.

This event includes:

- canoe races

- dances

- traditional songs

- storytelling

- and community gathering

It also reinforces an important truth:

Sasq'ets is not a mascot.Not a gimmick.Not a monster.

It is a being deeply woven into the identity of the land itself.

This cultural perspective gives Harrison a level of authenticity that no other Sasquatch hotspot can claim.

THE LANDSCAPE THAT HIDES GIANTS

To understand why Harrison remains so active, consider its terrain:

Endless mountain passes

These allow wide-ranging movement without ever entering human territory.

High alpine plateaus

Perfect for seasonal food sources.

Valleys that act as funnels

Animals — including Sasq'ets — follow natural corridors to water.

Lakes and rivers full of salmon

High-calorie food sources are crucial for large mammals.

Thick canopy

Ideal concealment.

Low human density

Even today, most of the land around the lake is unexplored.

Harrison isn't just a hotspot — it's a **biological stronghold**.

If Sasquatch exists anywhere, this is one of the few places where a breeding population could hide.

FIELD NOTES — CASE FILES OF THE HARRISON SYSTEM

Case File 5A — The Winter Tracks (2007)

Snowshoers discovered a line of enormous, human-like tracks crossing a frozen drainage.Stride measured at **54 inches** — impossible for a human.

Case File 5B — The Two Figures on the Ridge (2011)

A conservation officer reported seeing **two upright figures** walking a high ridge at dusk.He returned days later to find large tracks in snow near the summit.

Case File 5C — The Cabin Incident (2018)

A remote cabin north of Harrison recorded heavy knocks on the exterior walls at 3 a.m.Camera traps captured nothing — but one microphone picked up a low, resonant moan.

Analysts confirmed:**not bear, not cougar, not human.**

WHY HARRISON MATTERS TO THE BIGFOOT WORLD

Harrison Hot Springs is more than a backdrop for stories.It is the **center of gravity** for Sasquatch research in Canada.

Here, the worlds of:

- Indigenous knowledge

- settler encounters

- modern sightings

- ecological reality

- and field investigation

all overlap into something impossible to ignore.

This isn't a place where people ask *if* Sasquatch exists.

It's a place where people ask:

"Did you ever see him?""Where was it?""What did he look like?""How big was he?""Was he alone?""Did he follow you?"

The assumption — the default — is belief.

Not blind belief.Not naive belief.But **pragmatic belief** rooted in thousands of years of stories and a century of consistent sightings.

Harrison Hot Springs is not the birthplace of Sasquatch.

But it is the place where the rest of the worldfinally learned the name.

CHAPTER 6 — VANCOUVER ISLAND: FORESTS OF SHADOW & ECHO

There are places in Canada where the wilderness feels intimidating. Then there are places where the wilderness feels alive.

Vancouver Island belongs to the second category.

From the moment the ferry pushes away from the mainland and the coast begins to shrink behind you, something changes — not just in scenery, but in the air, the light, even the way sound moves through space. The Island has a presence. A depth. A weight. It's as if the land itself has a heartbeat.

And somewhere in that pulse — between the misty coastlines, the moss-draped forests, and the high mountain passes — live some of the strangest wilderness mysteries in British Columbia.

Bigfoot isn't a rare topic on Vancouver Island. It's woven into everything — into trail stories, logging camp folklore, Indigenous teachings, and the quiet things people whisper to you when you sit with them around a fire.

The Island's forests hold secrets. Some whispered. Some recorded. Some that still echo through the moss and the shadows.

This chapter is about the encounters that have shaped Vancouver Island's reputation as one of the most mysterious regions in Canada.

A LAND BUILT FOR MYSTERY

Vancouver Island is not a small island. People who've never been assume it's like Prince Edward Island — gentle, scenic, easy.

They're wrong.

It's a mountain range wrapped in ocean.A wall of rainforest against the Pacific.A labyrinth of old logging roads that twist into valleys where no human may set foot for years.A place where massive cedar stumps from the 1800s sit like forgotten monuments.

Everything here grows larger:

- the trees

- the ferns

- the silence

- the distance between communities

- the sense that the land goes on forever

And because of this, the Island behaves like a self-contained world, isolated even from mainland British Columbia—a place where evolution could follow its own path, where animals could thrive unseen, and where something big could vanish into the shade of a moss-covered ravine without leaving a trace.

It isn't hard to imagine a large primate surviving here.It's harder to imagine one *not* surviving here.

THE INDIGENOUS FOUNDATIONS — BEINGS OF THE COAST & MOUNTAINS

Vancouver Island is home to the Coast Salish, Nuu-chah-nulth, and Kwakwaka'wakw Nations—each with old stories about forest-dwelling beings that parallel Sasquatch accounts with uncanny precision.

Among the Nuu-chah-nulth, the T̲suw̲ha describe giant, hairy beings walking between mountain passes, avoiding humans but occasionally watching them from a distance.

Among the Kwakwa̱ka̱'wakw, the Dzunuk'wa—the Wild Woman of the Woods—is portrayed in masks not as a monster but as something powerful, ancient, and deeply rooted in reality.

Among the Coast Salish, stories of hairy people who lived deeper in the forests than humans did were never considered myths, but simple truths.

A line from one Elder captures the Island better than any scientific article ever could:

"This is not a place of stories.This is a place of memory."

In other words:**The beings people see here are not imaginary.They are part of the land.**

A PERSONAL IMPRESSION — THE FEELING OF VANCOUVER ISLAND

I've been to British Columbia several times, mostly Vancouver Island.I've traveled from the bottom to the top of it—through Sooke, Port Renfrew, Tofino, Nanaimo, Campbell River, and farther north into quiet logging towns where the roads feel like narrow ribbons lost in a dense green sea.

Every time I return, that first breath of west-coast air hits differently.Warmer. Wetter. Heavier.Carrying the scent of cedar, saltwater, and something older.

The whale-watching trip I took in the north remains one of my favourite memories:cold ocean wind, fog rolling like breath across the water, the sudden rise of a humpback's back breaking the surface, the sound it made—like an exhale from a creature that has lived through ten human lifetimes.

And everywhere, that sense of **awe and wonder**, as if the Island is aware of its own majesty.

But Vancouver Island also has shadow.

There are backroads where the trees lean in so tightly it feels like a tunnel, where daylight disappears, where the silence grows thick, where the hair on your arms stands up for reasons you can't explain.

When I visited several well-known sighting areas, I wasn't expecting to feel anything.But I did.

A pressure.A watchfulness.A presence at the treeline.

The Island's forest doesn't just surround you.It observes you.

THE OLD LOGGING ROADS — WHERE THE STORIES BEGIN

Some of the Island's most compelling accounts come from loggers who worked deep in the interior during the 1960s–1990s. Logging roads created temporary access into areas that had been untouched for centuries, and with that intrusion came encounters.

Many loggers told the same kinds of stories:

- **distant silhouettes** watching them from hillsides

- **heavy bipedal footsteps** around equipment left overnight

- **food supplies missing** without signs of bear behaviour

- **knocking sounds** echoing in patterns from ridge to ridge

- **massive prints** found in soft ground

- **rocks thrown** from the treeline at dusk

One old foreman, interviewed decades later, said:

"Every camp had a story.Every last one.Some guys didn't talk about it.Some talked too much.But nobody thought it was a joke."

Logging is practical work.Practical men do it.These weren't people prone to embellishment.They were people who knew the difference between wildlife and something else.

And Vancouver Island gave them something else.

THE SOOKE BASIN & PORT RENFREW — COASTAL SHADOW ZONES

The southern end of the Island, near Sooke and Port Renfrew, has one of the densest concentrations of sighting reports.

This region is famous for:

- sheer cliffs

- endless old-growth forest

- remote beaches

- steep river valleys

- fog that moves like living smoke

It is also famous for what the locals call **"coastal walkers"**—dark figures seen crossing beaches at dusk, moving along driftwood lines, or stepping between boulders where no person should be.

The Painter's Trail Encounter

In the early 1970s, a painter walking a narrow trail near Port Renfrew saw a large, upright figure crouched by the riverbank.It rose slowly, towering above the man, and walked into the trees.

No aggression.No chase.Just quiet recognition—on both sides.

The 1993 Campground Incident

A family camping near the Sooke Potholes woke to the sound of something large pacing around their tent.When the father shone a light outside, he saw a dark shape standing beside a tree, shoulders nearly as wide as the trunk.

When he yelled, it stepped back and vanished into the dark.

Rangers later examined massive footprints in soft sand near the river.

THE MID-ISLAND CORRIDOR — PARKSVILLE TO PORT ALBERNI

Inland Vancouver Island has its own reputation.The mountains around Port Alberni are riddled with reports from hikers, hunters, and backroad travelers.

Many describe:

- **whoops** echoing across valleys

- **knocks** that respond in perfect rhythm

- **shadow-like figures** watching from ridges

- **activity around campsites at night**

One pair of hikers reported seeing a tall, dark figure scramble effortlessly up a loose shale slope that took them half an hour to ascend.

Another case involved a set of footprints found along a logging road after a fresh snowfall — the prints moved in a straight line across terrain too rough for a human to navigate barefoot.

NORTHERN VANCOUVER ISLAND — THE RAW EDGE OF THE WORLD

If southern Vancouver Island feels old, northern Vancouver Island feels **primeval**.

Here the mountains close in tighter, the forests grow thicker, and the human footprint becomes sparse. Small communities like Port McNeill, Alert Bay, and Port Hardy sit on the margins of wilderness that stretches north into untouched country.

This is where some of the Island's most chilling sightings originate.

The Echo Bay Incident (1980s)

A fisherman repairing nets at dusk saw a massive figure step out of the treeline, kneel by the shore, and drink from the water using its cupped hands.The creature then looked toward the man before standing and walking into the forest.

The Knight Inlet Vocalization (2002)

Kayakers staying at a remote cabin recorded a long, rising howl late at night — unlike wolves, bears, or cougars.Audio experts later described it as "primate-like" but too large for any known species.

The Logging Road Stalker (2015)

A young hunter driving alone north of Woss saw a tall, dark figure cross the road in two steps.The figure paused at the treeline, turned its upper body, and stared at him before vanishing.

His words:

"It wasn't scared of me.It wanted me to see it."

That behaviour matches countless Ontario accounts as well.

THE STRANGENESS OF THE ISLAND — SILENCE, SHADOWS, AND PRESENCE

People who haven't been to Vancouver Island can't fully understand the feeling of its deep interior.

There are forests where:

- the air feels too still

- birds stop calling all at once

- fog sits low to the ground

- branches creak as if something heavy is moving in them

- time feels slower

- direction becomes harder to track

- the treeline feels like it's watching you

I've felt this myself.It's not imagination.

There are places on the Island where the wilderness feels… inhabited.

Not by humans.Not by known animals.By *something* else.

Something that does not want to be found,but does not want to be forgotten.

CASE FILES — VANCOUVER ISLAND

Case File 6A — The Beach Walker (1972)

A retired couple walking a remote beach at sunset saw a tall, lanky figure moving across the sand ahead of them.When they tried to approach, the figure slipped into the forest without a sound.

Case File 6B — The Logging Road Screams (1998)

Two truckers heard a series of deep, resonant screams echoing from a valley near Port Alberni.Both men described the sound as "too deep for any man, too powerful for any animal."

Case File 6C — The Tented Visitor (2019)

Campers near Nitinat Lake reported a hand pressing gently on the fabric of their tent at 3 a.m., fingers spread wide.Footprints around the site measured 16–18 inches.

WHY THE ISLAND MATTERS

Vancouver Island is not just another hotspot.

It is a self-contained world with:

- perfect habitat

- deep Indigenous knowledge

- consistent sightings

- historical accounts

- modern evidence

- and a long tradition of people encountering something they cannot explain

The Island's forests hold more than animals and plants.

They hold stories.Memories.Echoes.Presence.

And somewhere in those shadows,in the deep ravines and along the mist-covered rivers,a being walks that is older than the roads,older than the towns,older than the names we've given it.

On Vancouver Island, Bigfoot isn't a possibility.It's a neighbour you rarely see,but always feel.

CHAPTER 7 — BELLA COOLA & THE GREAT BEAR RAINFOREST

The Deep Valley Where Giants Still Walk

There are places in British Columbia where the wilderness feels ancient, and then there are places where it feels primordial — as if the world never fully moved past the age of giants. Bella Coola is one of those places. A deep, steep-sided valley carved by glaciers and framed by snow-hammered peaks, it is a land where the mountains don't just rise; they tower. They lean in. They swallow sound. They force you to look up and remember how small you really are.

If Vancouver Island feels like a world unto itself, Bella Coola feels like an entire era unto itself — a place caught between time and myth, where the line between "wilderness" and "presence" becomes razor thin. The locals feel it. The visitors feel it. The people who move there feel it their entire lives. And those who stay long enough, especially those who work the land, often find themselves encountering something that defies the boundaries of what we consider possible.

Bella Coola isn't just another Sasquatch hotspot. It is **one of the most important regions in the entire Pacific Northwest** for understanding how these beings move, behave, and interact with the land.

This chapter explores the valley, the surrounding Great Bear Rainforest, and the encounters that continue to define it as one of the most mysterious places in Canada.

The Valley of Echoes and Eyes

Driving into Bella Coola is an experience in itself. Highway 20 winds through the Chilcotin Plateau before dropping sharply into the valley in a series of steep, white-knuckle switchbacks known locally as **The Hill**.

These aren't simple twists in the road — they are a descent into a different world.

When you reach the bottom, the first thing you notice is **the silence**.

The valley absorbs sound the way deep snow absorbs footprints. And that silence can be unsettling. It feels full, alive, as though the trees themselves are listening.

The Nuxalk people, whose history in the valley goes back thousands of years, have always spoken of other beings in these forests — watchers, giants, forest guardians, and those who walk the ridgelines at night.

This isn't something they "believe."It's something they know.

The stories predate modern BC by centuries. And unlike other parts of Canada, where Indigenous and settler accounts sometimes diverge, in Bella Coola the stories are almost perfectly aligned.

Both describe:

- Tall, hair-covered beings

- Upright posture

- Silent movement

- No fear of steep terrain

- Long arms

- A calm, observational presence

- Deep, resonant calls echoing through valleys

If you're looking for an area where the old stories and modern sightings overlap without contradiction, this valley is unmatched.

An Ecosystem Built for Giants

The Great Bear Rainforest — stretching from Bella Coola toward the coast — is one of the last truly wild temperate rainforests on Earth. It has everything a large primate species could ever need:

- **Glacial rivers full of salmon**

- **Massive berry grounds**

- **Infinite escape routes** into steep terrain

- **Warm, sheltered valley bottoms**

- **High-elevation plateaus** rarely visited by humans

- **Coastal inlets** that allow movement between territories

For thousands of years, wildlife here has thrived because there is simply too much land for humans to monitor. Even today, the majority of the valley wall terrain is unreachable except by helicopter or multi-day climbs.

If there is any region in BC — or Canada — where a breeding population of Sasquatch could exist, Bella Coola is arguably one of the most likely candidates.

The Ridge-Walkers of the Nuxalkmc

Among the Nuxalk people, stories of **mountain giants** go back so far they are considered part of the valley's identity. These beings are not described as supernatural or imaginary. They are described as *physical*, *real*, and *occasionally interactive*.

Some Nuxalkmc hunters have spoken of:

- Giants watching them from across the valley

- Massive silhouettes moving along the top of cliffs

- Footsteps that shake loose shale from slopes

- Calls that vibrate through their chests

- Encounters that leave them shaken but unharmed

One Elder explained it simply:

"They live in the places we do not go."

This philosophy appears across many Indigenous cultures, including those in Ontario. The idea is not that the beings are hiding from humans, but that humans generally do not belong in the places where the beings live.

Bella Coola is full of those places.

The Famous Fisherman Encounter (1930s)

One of the earliest written accounts from the Bella Coola region comes from a fisherman who was checking his nets at dawn. As he moved along the riverbank, he saw a towering figure crouched on the opposite side of the water.

At first, he thought it was a bear. Then it stood up.

He described it as:

- Over seven feet tall

- Covered in dark brown hair

- With a broad, flat face

- Long arms reaching past the hips

The figure watched him silently before turning and walking into the trees.No aggression.No fear.Just awareness.

The fisherman reported the encounter to the RCMP, who investigated but found nothing conclusive.

Still, the story spread — not because it was sensational, but because so many Nuxalk families said the same thing:

"We have seen them there many times."

The River Guardian — A Multi-Generation Story

In the Bella Coola valley, there are stories passed through families of giants that follow salmon runs — appearing at river edges during spawning seasons, sometimes observing from the shadows and other times stepping openly into view.

One family reported encounters spanning **three generations**:

- A grandfather in the 1940s witnessed a tall figure wading through a shallow part of the Atnarko River.

- His son in the 1970s saw a similar figure standing knee-deep in the river, scooping fish with its hands.

- A grandson in the early 2000s reported hearing a deep, echoing call directly across the water from their campsite.

These aren't stories of monsters.They're stories of wildlife — except the wildlife is simply far larger and far more intelligent than any known animal.

The Logging Camp Incident (1960s)

During a remote road-building operation in the 1960s, loggers began reporting strange activity near their camp:

- Loud nighttime knocks

- Stones thrown toward equipment

- Deep moaning calls echoing off the valley walls

- Heavy footsteps around the perimeter

One worker claimed a massive figure briefly emerged from the treeline before disappearing again.

Another claimed something with long arms reached into the camp's refuse pit at night.

An old foreman later said:

"We weren't scared of bears.But whatever was out there wasn't a bear."

Logging crews are practical people. They know what wildlife looks like. When they say something was wrong, it usually was.

The Modern Sightings — Still Happening Today

Bella Coola remains one of the most active Sasquatch regions in BC.

The 2003 Sightline Encounter

A bowhunter sitting quietly on a ridge watched a dark figure move between trees below him.He initially thought it was another hunter in dark clothing.But then the figure stepped into a clearing and stood nearly eight feet tall.

He froze.It froze.They watched each other for several seconds before the figure turned and walked uphill with unnatural speed.

His account:

"I've hunted bears my whole life.That was no bear.Its arms were too long, its body too narrow, its walk too smooth."

The Valley Road Crossing (2010s)

A highway worker driving at dawn saw a tall figure cross the road in front of his truck.He braked hard.The figure turned its torso — not its head — to look at him.

It took three strides to cross the asphalt.

Three strides.

The Riverbed Tracks (2021)

A pair of hikers found massive, human-shaped footprints in a muddy riverbed after heavy rain.Stride: over four feet.Depth: significantly deeper than theirs.No toe claw marks.

When they posted the photos, locals reacted calmly:

"They've been here forever.This isn't new."

That reaction speaks volumes.

Nuxalk Teachings — Where the Beings Live

The Nuxalkmc distinguish between:

- **Spirit beings** (supernatural entities)

- **Forest beings** (physical, living creatures)

Sasquatch — known in parts of their tradition as **Boqs** or **Bukwus** depending on context — is considered physical.

Elders describe them as:

- intelligent

- strong

- elusive

- protective of certain areas

- capable of communicating intent

- avoidant but not fearful

One Elder once said:

"They know the valley better than we do.They have their own paths."

This aligns perfectly with sightings where the beings seem to appear and disappear effortlessly, as if using trails invisible to humans.

A Valley of Vanishings

Though this book is not yet focused on disappearances, Bella Coola's wilderness has its share of missing-hunter and missing-hiker cases — many with odd elements:

- sudden weather changes

- silent forests at the time of vanishing

- search dogs losing scent abruptly

- gear found neatly placed

Some cases hint at being classic wilderness misfortunes.Others fit patterns familiar to researchers.

Bella Coola has a long history of people disappearing — not in great numbers, but in strange, quiet, unsettling ways that echo other parts of British Columbia and the far north.

When you walk these forests, you understand why.

There are places where the wilderness feels too aware.Too silent.Too heavy.

And sometimes, too crowded.

CASE FILES — BELLA COOLA & THE GREAT BEAR

Case File 7A — The Three Shadows (1998)

A fisherman cleaning gear at dusk saw three tall silhouettes standing on a rock outcropping above the river.When he raised his light, the figures stepped backward into the trees simultaneously — coordinated, deliberate.

Case File 7B — The Cliff-Side Walker (2007)

A hiker spotted a dark figure walking effortlessly along a narrow cliff edge hundreds of feet above the valley floor.No human could traverse that slope safely.

Case File 7C — The Campsite Visitor (2016)

Campers heard heavy, bipedal footsteps surrounding their campsite.One placed a hand outside the tent and felt something brush against him — coarse hair.

He didn't leave the tent again until morning.

The Mystery of Bella Coola

Bella Coola is the kind of place that reminds you the world is still large enough to hide secrets — and that some secrets prefer to stay hidden.

The valley feels like a living chamber.The mountains feel like guardians.The air feels ancient.The forests feel occupied.

There are places in Canada where you *suspect* Sasquatch may exist.There are places where stories persist.Places where sightings cluster.Places where evidence appears.

But Bella Coola is different.

Bella Coola is a place where, if you listen long enough,you start to feel like the forest is trying to tell you something.

And maybe—just maybe—something is listening back.

CHAPTER 8 — THE INTERIOR PLATEAU: KAMLOOPS, CARIBOO & THE HIGH COUNTRY
Where the Grasslands Meet the Deep Forest

There are parts of British Columbia where the wilderness feels like an unbroken wall of green — endless rainforest stretching from valley floor to snowy ridge. The Interior Plateau is different. It is a shifting world of forests, open grasslands, sagebrush basins, and rolling mountains that stretch for hundreds of kilometres. A place that feels vast and layered, like you're driving across the back of a sleeping continent.

It's also a place where some of the most unusual, credible, and deeply unsettling Sasquatch encounters have been recorded in Canadian history.

Unlike the coastal sightings — where dense forest obscures most of the land — here the openness of the terrain means witnesses often get **clear views**, long-distance comparisons, and prolonged encounters.

The Interior Plateau is often overlooked in mainstream Bigfoot discussions, overshadowed by Vancouver Island and the coast. But talk to ranchers, loggers, hunters, or First Nations Elders from the region, and you'll quickly discover this:

The Interior Plateau is one of the strongest Sasquatch hotspots in British Columbia — and always has been.

A Land Built for Movement

What makes the plateau unique is how easy it is for a large animal to move through it.

Unlike the steep, barrier-filled valleys of the coast, the Interior Plateau:

- has **gentle elevations**

- contains massive **grassland corridors**

- sits between mountain ranges

- features an enormous **network of game trails**

- has thousands of kilometres of **logging roads**

- offers **diverse ecosystems** only minutes apart

This region is essentially a natural highway system for wildlife — and for anything else moving through the land.

Deer, elk, moose, black bear, and grizzlies use these corridors constantly. Ranchers see predators crossing open fields. Hunters track movement along ridgelines for kilometres.

And if Sasquatch exists as a physical being — something that needs space, food, and travel efficiency — the Interior Plateau is a paradise.

This is where sightings become clearer, more detailed, and more behaviourally consistent.

Kamloops — The City with a Hidden History

Kamloops sits at the meeting of two rivers and several ecosystems. The region is dry, rugged, and sunny — the last place people imagine when they picture Sasquatch habitat.

And yet, Kamloops and its surrounding hills have produced **more sightings than most BC cities**.

Locals talk about:

- tall, dark figures seen at dusk above the Thompson River

- rock-throwing incidents on remote hiking trails

- strange calls echoing through grassland canyons

- massive prints found near dirt-bike trails

- cattle spooked for no identifiable reason

- highway sightings along Route 1, 5, and 97

One Kamloops hunter said:

"People assume Bigfoot lives in rainforest. But he likes these hills. You can see everything from up here."

Many sightings occur just outside town:

The Bachelor Hills Encounter

A man walking his dog near sunset saw a tall figure standing in the sagebrush, still as a post. The dog froze, growled, then hid behind his legs — something it had never done.

When the man yelled, the figure turned and walked uphill with long, powerful strides.

Knox Mountain Lookout (Early 2000s)

Two mountain bikers riding a ridge heard a series of sharp knocks echoing across the valley. Then came a deep, resonant whoop.

They stopped and listened. The sound answered itself several times — coming from two different directions.

Whatever made the call moved fast.

The Cariboo — Land of Loggers, Ranchers & Old Stories

The Cariboo region — stretching from Clinton to Quesnel — is a place where frontier history still feels fresh. Ranches sit on land that hasn't changed much since the 1800s. Logging trucks rattle down dirt roads that lead to long-forgotten valleys. Lakes and rivers weave through forests that seem endless at times.

And in all of that, witnesses describe encounters with an animal that has no business existing — unless it has always been here.

The Clinton Corridor

Highway 97 between Clinton and 70 Mile House is one of the most sighted stretches of road in the Interior Plateau.

Dozens of reports describe:

- tall, dark figures crossing the road

- silhouettes standing at treelines

- deer fleeing from something unseen

- calls at night that shake truck campers

One trucker reported seeing a figure nearly eight feet tall step onto the highway, pause, and then retreat into the woods.

He described the movement as:

"Too smooth for a bear. Too fast for a human. Too damn big for either."

Williams Lake & Surrounding Forests

Williams Lake is known for ranching and rodeo culture — not for cryptids.But the deeper you go into the forest, the more the stories surface.

Hunters describe hearing long, powerful calls at dusk.Families camping off old logging roads have heard knocks echoing from ridge to ridge.Some ranchers have claimed cattle vanish without a trace — not wolves, not cougars.

One rancher said he saw a tall figure watching his herd from a distant hill.He rode out to investigate, but the figure disappeared in seconds.

When he reached the hilltop, the grass was flattened where something large had knelt.

He said:

"It was watching them like a man watches a herd."

Deadman Valley — One of BC's Forgotten Hotspots

Deadman Valley sits northwest of Savona and has long been considered one of the Interior Plateau's most active regions.

The terrain is ideal:

- rolling hills

- thick timber

- isolated ranches

- old mining trails

- steep ravines perfect for concealment

And the sightings go back decades.

The Trapper's Encounter (1970s)

A trapper walking along a creek noticed movement on the hillside.He raised his binoculars and saw a tall, hair-covered figure crouched near a cluster of rocks.

The figure then stood, looked down the hill toward him, and walked away — uphill — with a stride too long for any human.

He later said:

"It walked like it owned the place.I felt like I was trespassing."

The Deadman Road Footprint Series (Late 1990s)

A family driving a backroad spotted large footprints in a patch of mud.They stopped, measured them, and found prints over **17 inches long** with a four-foot stride.

The tracks crossed the road and vanished into the bushes.

A conservation officer examined the photos and said, carefully:

"Those aren't bear."

Lillooet & the High Country — The Old Gold Routes

Lillooet is steeped in history — gold rush trails, prospectors, and cattle drives. It's also steeped in mystery.

Hunters in the region describe:

- massive prints found near high-elevation lakes

- vocalizations echoing across alpine basins

- boulder-sized rocks thrown into water

- encounters at tree line where something watched from the shadows

One mountain hunter found a shelter made of broken pine limbs woven together in a way no bear or windstorm could replicate.

The structure was nearly eight feet tall.

Bonaparte Plateau — A Perfect Environment

Between Cache Creek and Kamloops sits the Bonaparte Plateau — a flat, forested expanse full of lakes, marshes, and thick timber.

This region might be one of the most ideal Sasquatch habitats in the entire Interior Plateau.

The Moose Hunter's Encounter (2004)

A hunter tracking a bull moose saw a tall, dark figure step onto a distant ridge.It watched him for nearly a full minute — unmoving, silent.

The hunter raised his rifle scope, then immediately lowered it.

He said:

"I felt like aiming at it was a bad idea.It knew what a rifle was.That scared me more than anything."

Morning Trackway Discovery

A group of fishermen found a line of human-shaped tracks along a muddy lakeshore at dawn.The tracks were so fresh the edges were still collapsing.

No human had walked there — the ground was too soft and too remote.

Stride: nearly **four feet**.

First Nations Perspectives — The Watchers of the High Country

The Secwepemc and Tsilhqot'in peoples have stories going back generations describing beings that:

- walk the hills at dusk

- travel along ancient ridgelines

- watch hunters from a distance

- follow salmon runs along rivers

- live in the high country where humans rarely go

These beings are **not monsters**, not legends, not myths — but a part of the land.

One Elder explained:

"They travel where the deer travel,but they see farther than we do."

These accounts perfectly match the modern sightings.

The Interior Plateau Soundscape — A Different Kind of Quiet

Anyone who has hunted or camped in the plateau knows the sound:

- wind in the grass

- dry rattle of sage

- distant coyote calls

- the sharp snap of a twig

- the sudden silence that follows

That silence is what witnesses describe most often.

They say the quiet becomes:

- deeper

- heavier

- unnatural

- like something is holding its breath

And then — from the forest, a single knock.Or a rhythmic series of them.Or a long call that rolls across the hills like thunder softened by distance.

Some describe a sense of being **observed**, not stalked — watched the way a predator watches other predators.

The land feels too open for secrets.But the forests feel like they're full of them.

Case Files — The Interior Plateau

Case File 8A — The Midnight Road Crosser (Highway 97, 2011)

A trucker driving between Clinton and Prince George saw a tall figure cross the road in three steps.Its silhouette was clearly defined in the headlights.It never looked at him — it simply moved into the forest.

Case File 8B — The Riverbend Screams (Chilcotin, 1990s)

Campers heard deep, resonant screams echoing from across the river.The calls repeated, louder each time.A bear wandered into camp afterward — unusually agitated.

Case File 8C — The Hunting Blind Visitor (Kamloops, early 2000s)

A hunter sitting silently in a blind smelled a strong, musky odour moments before heavy bipedal footsteps circled behind him.He never saw the creature.But he left the blind and never returned to that valley.

Why the Interior Plateau Matters

This region gives us something rare in Bigfoot research:

Sightings with clarity.Sightings with distance.Sightings with detail.

The open terrain allows for longer visual contact.The hills create echo chambers for calls and knocks.The wildlife corridors support movement.The forests offer concealment.The grasslands offer vantage points.

And the people who live here — loggers, ranchers, hunters — know the land intimately.

When they say something isn't a bear,isn't a human,isn't a trick of light…

They mean it.

The Interior Plateau is where the mystery stops being speculative and starts becoming observable.

A region where the land itself feels like a witness —holding stories in every ridge, every sagebrush basin, every quiet forest trail.

A region where something still walks.Something large.Something intelligent.Something that has lived here longer than the roads, the ranches, and the people who now call this place home.

CHAPTER 9 — THE FRASER CANYON: STEEP WALLS & SHADOWED HISTORIES
Where the River Cuts Deep and the Stories Run Deeper

There are stretches of British Columbia that feel dangerous because of wildlife, weather, or isolation. The Fraser Canyon feels dangerous because of **presence**.

It isn't a passive landscape.It isn't a place you merely pass through.It's a place that looms, tightens, swallows you into its narrow throat, and watches you the entire time.

The Fraser Canyon is raw, towering, and ancient — a corridor carved by the relentless force of the Fraser River crashing through rock that predates human history. It is a place where the mountains lean in so steeply that the sky becomes a thin ribbon overhead. Where railways cling to cliffs like stubborn afterthoughts. Where tunnels, bridges, and carved ledges feel like temporary intrusions into a land that existed long before people arrived.

And somewhere along those sheer walls, hidden plateaus, and shadowed forests are some of the oldest and most credible Sasquatch encounters ever documented.

This region is the **spine** of British Columbia — a natural passageway connecting the coast to the interior. Animals have used it for thousands of years. Humans have used it for thousands more. And according to Indigenous Nations, the **Sasq'ets** have walked it since time immemorial.

This chapter explores the encounters, the history, and the strange sense of being watched that follows you through every bend.

A Corridor Built for Movement — And for Silence

What makes the Fraser Canyon remarkable is its shape.

It is not a wide valley like Bella Coola or the Cariboo. It is a narrow, steep-walled trench running north-south, funnelling:

- wildlife

- weather

- sound

- and anything that travels on two legs

through its confined space.

And yet, even with the closeness of the terrain, it's shockingly easy for a large animal to slip out of sight.

Every cliff has ledges. Every slope has pockets of forest. Every canyon wall hides small plateaus just out of view. The train lines and highways touch only the bottom edge — the rest is endless vertical wilderness.

You can stand on the shoulder of Highway 1 and hear a knock echo from the cliffs with no idea where it originated.

You can hike only a few minutes off a recreation trail and find yourself completely hidden from passing vehicles.

This is the essence of Sasquatch territory.

It is also a place where witnesses have described some of the clearest, closest encounters in BC history.

Yale — The Historical Epicenter

To understand the Fraser Canyon, you must start in **Yale**, one of the oldest and most culturally significant towns in British Columbia.

Yale was once a booming gold rush town — a frontier settlement bursting with miners, traders, and people passing in and out of the wilderness. It was here, in the late 1800s and early 1900s, that some of the earliest settler accounts of large, hairy wild people began circulating.

Reports from the time describe:

- enormous footprints along riverbanks

- strange screams echoing from forested slopes

- miners seeing tall figures around campfires

- prospectors being watched from ridgelines

- supplies going missing without typical animal signs

These weren't the exaggerated newspaper hoaxes that plagued other regions.They were simple testimonies, often from hardened men who rarely exaggerated anything.

And underneath these accounts were much older stories — Kawakawa Lake traditions, Nlaka'pamux legends, Stó:lō teachings — all speaking of forest giants inhabiting the canyon long before the gold rush.

One Elder said:

"People think the Sasq'ets came with the settlers.No.The settlers came to where the Sasq'ets already lived."

The Lady Franklin Rock Sightings

Lady Franklin Rock is a famous landmark near Yale — a tall stone pillar rising from the river.Over the years, people crossing the nearby rail line or driving along the canyon have reported figures moving on the slopes above the rock.

In the late 1940s, a rail crew reported seeing a tall, dark silhouette watching them from a ledge 40 feet above the tracks.

One crew member said:

"It was too big to be a man.Too upright to be a bear.And too calm to be either."

The figure remained still as the train passed.When the men returned with more workers an hour later, it was gone — but fresh prints were found in the loose gravel.

Hell's Gate — A Place That Feels Alive

Hell's Gate is one of the most dramatic sights in British Columbia.The river narrows violently, exploding between steep walls of rock with a thunderous roar that drowns everything but the loudest sounds.

Visitors describe Hell's Gate as beautiful.Locals describe it as unsettling.

There have been reports of:

- knocks echoing between canyon walls

- screams rising above the roar of the river

- large figures seen on cliffs near dusk

- footprints on the sandy shoreline below observation decks

One fisherman recalls seeing something crouched near the water's edge early one morning, scooping at the river with a long arm.

When he approached, the figure moved away, climbing the rocks in a way no human could.

He said the strangest part was how quiet it moved:

"The river was so loud it should've drowned everything out.But I swear I heard its footsteps."

Boston Bar & North Bend — The Twin Hotspots

Boston Bar and North Bend sit across the river from each other, surrounded by steep mountainsides and dense forest.

Residents here have decades of stories.Not rumours — accounts.Not campfire tales — memories.

The North Bend Logging Road Encounter (1970s)

Several loggers working late heard rhythmic knocking echoing from the forest.They assumed it was another crew signaling something.

Then the knocking began behind them —followed by a low, resonant hoot.

Tools were dropped.Engines were shut off.Everyone listened.

The sound came again — louder, deeper.

A foreman described it as:

"A voice too big for any human throat."

The Boston Bar Road Crosser (Early 2000s)

A couple driving north at dusk saw a towering figure step onto the road.Their headlights hit it full on.

They described:

- a tall body covered in dark brown hair

- a conical head shape

- arms nearly to the knees

- a calm, almost deliberate pace

It did not run.It did not appear startled.It simply crossed the road, then stepped over the guardrail and disappeared into the trees.

The couple were so shaken they drove directly to the Boston Bar RCMP detachment.The officer on duty listened carefully, then quietly said they were not the first to report such a sighting in that area.

Nahatlatch Valley — One of BC's Hidden Gems

Few outsiders know the Nahatlatch Valley even exists.

Those who do rarely forget it.

Nahatlatch Lake sits inside a hidden corridor of mountains and thick forest — a place where people camp, fish, and occasionally hear things they cannot explain.

The 2014 Lakeshore Encounter

A pair of campers sitting by their fire heard heavy footsteps above them on the hillside.At first, they assumed it was a deer.

Then came a deep, slow exhale —a sound like a massive chest releasing air.

The couple froze.Moments later, they heard something move downslope — heavy, bipedal — before the sound stopped abruptly.

One camper described feeling "pinned," like eyes were fixed on their site.

They slept in their vehicle that night.

The Canyon That Watches You Back

The Fraser Canyon has a particular atmosphere — one that many witnesses try to describe but never fully capture.

They say:

- the air feels heavier

- the silence feels deeper

- the shadows feel occupied

- the cliffs feel like they're holding secrets

- the hair on your neck rises for no logical reason

This isn't paranoia.It's pattern.

Numerous witnesses describe the sensation of being watched before any sound or movement occurs. Only afterward do they see a figure or hear a call. It's the same instinct prey animals have — the sense of an unseen predator.

And yet, in the canyon, the presence doesn't feel aggressive.Just observant.

Calm.Quiet.Ancient.

A Hiker's Account (2019)

A solo hiker near Alexandra Bridge described feeling watched for over an hour.When she finally turned around at a bend in the trail, she saw a tall figure at the treeline.

She said:

"It wasn't close enough to scare me.It was far enough to let me know it could've been closer if it wanted to."

This type of behaviour — non-aggressive observation — is common across BC.

Indigenous Knowledge — The Canyon People

The Stó:lō, Nlaka'pamux (Thompson), and St'at'imc peoples all have stories of large forest beings that inhabit the steep, forested slopes of the canyon.

These beings are described as:

- powerful

- intelligent

- solitary

- watchers

- guardians of certain river sections

Elders rarely discuss these stories in sensational terms.They describe them matter-of-factly.

One Elder said:

"They live in the high places where we do not go.Only sometimes do they travel low."

Another said:

"They've been here since the beginning.We pass through their home when we use the canyon."

This perspective changes the entire tone of Sasquatch research in the canyon:

It is not a matter of "if."It is a matter of **respect**.

Case Files — Fraser Canyon

Case File 9A — The Tunnel Watcher (1950s)

Rail workers reported a tall figure standing near the entrance of a rail tunnel at dusk.When approached, it stepped into the dark and vanished before lights could be shone inside.

Case File 9B — The Canyon Screams (1980s)

Campers near a pullout heard three powerful screams echoing from the opposite wall.Not cougar.Not bear.Not human.Each scream reverberated so strongly they felt it in their chests.

Case File 9C — The Ridge Silhouette (2012)

A group of kayakers saw a tall figure walking along a ridge above the river.The figure walked smoothly along terrain so steep the kayakers couldn't believe it was trying to stay balanced — until they realized:

It wasn't trying.

Why the Fraser Canyon Matters

The canyon is more than a series of rock walls and river bends.It is a natural highway that has guided movement for millennia:

- salmon

- bears

- wolves

- humans

- and possibly something else

The sightings here are not vague.They are often shockingly clear, visual, prolonged.

And they come from:

- loggers

- train workers

- RCMP

- hikers

- commuters

- Indigenous witnesses

- ranchers

- fishermen

A wide spectrum of credible observers.

The Fraser Canyon forces us to confront the possibility that Sasquatch is not a fringe myth but a long-standing resident of British Columbia's oldest travel corridor.

A being that has watched humans travel this canyon for thousands of years — from canoes to gold rush pack trains, from steam engines to semi-trucks.

A being that walks the same routes, moves through the same terrain, and sometimes steps close enough to remind us:

This valley does not belong to us. We are only passing through.

CHAPTER 10 — THE SUNSHINE COAST & SECHELT PENINSULA
Where Quiet Forests Hold Loud Secrets

There's a certain softness to the Sunshine Coast — the kind of calm, Pacific light that seems to hang in the air like a gentle haze. Ferries glide across still water. Small towns nestle along rocky shorelines. Coffee shops hum with a relaxed coastal rhythm. It doesn't feel like wilderness in the immediate sense. Not at first. Not in the way the Great Bear Rainforest or the Fraser Canyon does.

But step even a few minutes off the road — really step into the woods — and everything shifts.

The forests darken.The sound deepens.The trees grow massive and moss-laden.The air grows still.And the sense of being alone vanishes.

The Sunshine Coast isn't rugged in the way most people imagine British Columbia.It's deceptive.Beautiful.Welcoming.And yet, beneath that calm exterior lies a region with one of the most quietly consistent Bigfoot histories in the province.

The locals know.The Elders know.The hikers know.The hunters know.And in some cases, the creatures themselves seem aware of just how close humans live beside them.

This is a land of islands, peninsulas, bays, hidden valleys, logging roads, and dense second-growth forests. It's a region where encounters feel *personal* — not distant silhouettes across river canyons, but moments where something steps close enough to let you know it's real.

A Coast of Contrasts — Calm Shorelines, Deep Forest Interiors

The Sunshine Coast stretches from Langdale Ferry Terminal up to Powell River, carved by inlets, old logging roads, and mountains rising sharply from the sea.

The terrain shifts constantly:

- open seashores

- rocky bluffs

- thick cedar forests

- old-growth pockets hidden in valleys

- second-growth forests regenerating thick and fast

- steep mountains rising almost vertically from the water

This landscape creates two very different environments:

1. **Human spaces** — towns, seaside trails, weekend campsites.2. **Sasquatch spaces** — the shadowed, mossy, nearly impenetrable interiors.

And the boundary between the two is razor thin.

You can walk from a coffee shop patio into genuine wilderness in under ten minutes.And that's exactly why the encounters here often feel *close*.

As one local put it:

"You don't go into the deep forest here.The deep forest comes to you."

Sechelt — A Peninsula of Old Stories

The Sechelt Peninsula is one of the oldest cultural landscapes on the west coast. The shíshálh Nation (Sechelt Nation) has lived here for thousands of years, and their oral histories include beings that match the physical and behavioural descriptions of Sasquatch nearly perfectly.

These beings are described as:

- tall

- powerful

- hair-covered

- nocturnal

- territorial

- watchers of trails and waterways

- protectors of certain valleys

The Sechelt people have never framed these beings as "monsters."They are simply another part of the land.

Some Elders say that long ago, humans and these forest beings shared the region — not in harmony, but in mutual respect.

One Elder summarized it simply:

"They keep to the shade.We keep to the light.But our paths cross."

In the Sechelt backcountry, those paths cross more often than most realize.

The Hidden Logging Roads — Pathways Into the Unknown

Behind Sechelt, Roberts Creek, Halfmoon Bay, and Pender Harbour is a massive network of logging roads — some active, others long overgrown.

These roads lead into:

- deep, quiet valleys

- secluded lakes

- old-growth pockets hidden from public trails

- ridgelines with almost no human traffic

- forest meadows with abundant wildlife

And these are the areas where many Sunshine Coast encounters occur.

Hunters speak of:

- **knocks** that echo from ridge to ridge

- **long whoops** rolling down forested valleys

- **black silhouettes** stepping across distant logging cuts

- **heavy footsteps** paralleling them in the trees

- **massive prints** found in old skid trails

One hunter described hearing something "walk beside him" for nearly half an hour — always staying just out of view, always matching his pace.

He said:

"It wasn't trying to scare me.It was letting me know it was there."

That type of behaviour shows up repeatedly in BC's coastal encounters.

Roberts Creek — A Quiet Hotspot

Roberts Creek is known for coastal beauty, yoga retreats, surf culture, and a laid-back creative community.

It's *not* known publicly for Sasquatch activity.But locals have been reporting unusual encounters for decades.

The 1980s Night Walker

Several families living near the creek reported hearing something massive walking behind their properties at night.Dogs hid inside.Footsteps were slow, deliberate, heavy — too heavy for a person.

No property damage, no aggression — just movement.

The Backyard Watcher (Late 1990s)

A woman living on a rural property saw a tall figure standing near the treeline watching her from between two cedars.

When she shouted, the figure stepped backward and vanished into the dark.

She refused to walk the forest edge alone afterward.

The 2014 Trail Encounter

A trail runner saw a dark, upright shape crouched beside a log off-trail.When he stopped, the shape rose to its full height — far taller than any man — and walked uphill into dense brush without a sound.

He never returned to the trail alone.

Pender Harbour & Egmont — Where the Forest Reaches the Water

The northern Sunshine Coast becomes wilder as you travel up the peninsula. Pender Harbour and Egmont are surrounded by deep bays, complex coastlines, and dense forest that seems to grow right out of the rock.

The combination of ocean access and secluded terrain creates the perfect environment for a wide-ranging, intelligent animal.

The Fisherman's Encounter (1990s)

A fisherman cleaning his boat late at night heard heavy walking on the rocks above the marina.Expecting a black bear, he grabbed a flashlight and shone it toward the sound.

Two glowing, amber-coloured eyes reflected back — six to seven feet above the ground.

The figure turned and walked into the forest without breaking stride.

He said the shoulders were "wider than the doorframe of his boat."

The Morris Creek Footprints (2008)

A pair of teenagers found massive footprints in sand near a creek feeding into the harbour.The prints were so far apart that one boy tried jumping the distance — and couldn't land it.

The RCMP were shown photographs and reportedly told the family:

"We get calls like this from time to time.Just be aware in the area."

Powell River — The Quiet Giant of Sunshine Coast Research

North of Sechelt lies **Powell River**, a community surrounded by lakes, mountains, and deep wilderness. If Vancouver Island has shadowed forests and Bella Coola has ancient corridors, Powell River has endless forgotten terrain.

This region is packed with stories — many unreported publicly.

The Inland Lake Runner (Early 2000s)

A jogger on the Inland Lake Trail heard a rhythmic stomping behind him.Not running — **pounding**, like something with massive weight was keeping pace through the trees.

He heard it for over two minutes before it stopped abruptly.

He later said:

"It sounded like something was testing my pace."

The Dinner Plate Boulder Incident (2013)

Campers at Haslam Lake reported a boulder — roughly the size of a dinner plate — thrown into the water near their kayaks at dusk.

The splash was so large they initially thought it was an animal jumping in.

There were no cliffs nearby.No campers upstream.No boats.

And no human could have thrown a rock that size that far.

The Gourlay Bay Sighting (2016)

Kayakers spotted a tall, dark figure moving between shoreline boulders.They assumed it was a fisherman until it stepped fully upright and disappeared behind a large cedar stump.

They paddled closer, but whatever it was had vanished into the forest.

Indigenous Knowledge — The Shade Walkers

The shíshálh Nation has some of the most compelling oral teachings in the region.

These beings are known as:

- guardians of valleys

- watchers of trails

- protectors of water sources

- beings that dwell in the deep shade

They are not framed as malevolent.But they are not framed as harmless either.

They are framed as **ancient**.

One Elder said:

"They walk where we do not.They watch what we do not see."

Another noted that certain lakes and valleys should be respected because "you are not alone there."

These teachings align closely with sightings:

- encounters at lakeshores

- watchers near trails

- figures moving along shadowed ridges

- nighttime footsteps near camps

- massive prints appearing in areas with no recent human activity

The overlap between oral tradition and modern encounters is nearly perfect.

The Coast That Hides Its Secrets Well

The Sunshine Coast has a strange dual nature:

Publicly, it feels calm, welcoming, peaceful.**Privately**, it contains some of the most unnerving, consistent Sasquatch behaviour in British Columbia.

Witnesses describe:

- being followed on quiet trails

- hearing long, deep calls at dusk

- finding twisted branches or peeled bark

- discovering fresh tracks

- hearing bipedal footsteps on mossy ground

- sudden silence in bird-rich forests

- heavy breathing just out of sight

A wildlife photographer once said:

"You don't go looking for anything here.Whatever is here finds you."

This is why the Sunshine Coast is one of BC's most quietly active regions.

Not because sightings are loud.But because the land itself is so quiet that anything out of place becomes amplified.

The creatures seem to know that, too.

Case Files — Sunshine Coast & Sechelt Peninsula

Case File 10A — The Night Creek Screams (Roberts Creek, 1997)

Residents heard a powerful scream roll through the valley around 2 a.m.Several dogs refused to go outside.The scream was described as "too long and too deep for any known animal."

Case File 10B — The Forest Edge Watcher (Sechelt, 2005)

A man retrieving firewood saw a tall figure standing at the edge of his property, half-shadowed behind a cedar tree.It stepped backward and disappeared silently.

Case File 10C — The Trail Follower (Powell River, 2018)

A hiker felt he was being followed along a ridge trail.He later found large footprints in soft dirt — aligned perfectly with his own trail, just inside the treeline.

Why the Sunshine Coast Matters

The region doesn't announce itself the way Bella Coola or the Fraser Canyon does.It doesn't shout its mysteries.It whispers them.

And yet:

- sightings are close

- encounters are personal

- behaviour is consistent

- Indigenous teachings match modern reports

- tracks appear in areas minutes from town

- campers experience nighttime activity

- hunters hear knocks and whoops deep in the backcountry

This is a region where Sasquatch interacts with the land in subtle, quiet ways —but the consistency of those interactions is impossible to ignore.

The Sunshine Coast feels peaceful on the surface.But look closer, listen deeper, and you'll find a story unfolding:

A story of watchers.A story of shadowed forests.A story of something old, quiet, and aware.

A presence that moves along the peninsula,slipping between bays and lakes,crossing logging roads at dusk,and watching from the treeline as people walk along the shoreline unaware.

A presence that has likely lived here longer than the communities themselves.

And whether people believe in it or not,the forests of the Sunshine Coast hold secrets waiting to be told.

CHAPTER 11 — OGOPOGO: THE GUARDIAN OF OKANAGAN Lake

N'ha-a-itk: The Spirit That Never Left

The first time you stand on the shores of Okanagan Lake, it doesn't feel like any other lake in British Columbia.There's a presence to it — a quiet weight in the air, like the water itself is watching. Locals feel it, tourists sense it without knowing why, and for generations the Syilx (Okanagan) People have said the same thing:

This is not just a lake. This is a home. A territory. A boundary line. And something ancient lives beneath the surface.

Before there was "Ogopogo," there was **N'ha-a-itk**, a being as old as the valley itself — a guardian spirit, a powerful entity tied to the water, the cliffs, and the people who lived along the shoreline long before colonization.

When I started researching the mysteries of British Columbia, this lake stood out.Not just because of the monster stories, but because the phenomenon here is *consistent*.Hundreds of witnesses, decades of sonar hits, thousands of photographs — most useless, some compelling — and a cultural tradition that treats the creature as something far more complex than a Nessie-style animal.

Okanagan Lake is deep, narrow, and cold.Perfect for hiding something that doesn't want to be found.And after spending time here, talking with locals, walking the beaches at dusk, and hearing the stories firsthand, I believe that "Ogopogo" is only half the tale.

This lake has a memory.And something in it remembers us too.

The Origin: N'ha-a-itk, the Sacred Water Spirit (Before 1900)

Western pop culture turned Ogopogo into a cartoon — a green, smiling serpent used for tourism posters and kids' rides.But that version has nothing to do with the **Syilx** traditions the creature comes from.

In their stories, N'ha-a-itk wasn't a monster.It was a **guardian** — a protector of the valley, a defender of the land who demanded respect.

The stories vary, but many center around:

- A **powerful spirit** connected to the lake

- A being capable of defending its territory

- A creature associated with sudden storms or drowned travelers

- A force you didn't challenge lightly

One of the most famous stories tells of a local man, **Chief Timbasket**, who attempted to cross the lake without making the proper offering.N'ha-a-itk allegedly responded with fury, overturning his canoe and pulling him beneath the water.

This wasn't an animal acting on instinct.It was a being enforcing a rule.

Another early account describes fishermen seeing something **massive** rise from the water near Rattlesnake Island — long before settlers built homes along the lakeshore.

Colonial newspapers ignored the spiritual context and instead focused on the beast itself.By the 1910s, settlers were calling it:

- The "Okanagan Lake Serpent"

- The "Demon of the Deep"

- "The Water Ghost"

By the 1920s, a music hall jingle turned it into "Ogopogo," and the legend exploded.

Yet even today, Syilx elders say the creature is misunderstood.

"It is not a snake," one elder told a researcher in the 1970s. "It is not an animal you can hunt. It is a spirit. It has always been here."

And when you look at the sightings with that in mind, everything changes.

Modern Sightings — The Consistency That Shouldn't Exist

People see strange things on lakes all the time. Wind, wakes, shadows, boats — most reports are just that.

But Okanagan Lake is different.

Many sightings have nothing to do with waves or logs. They involve structured shapes, distinct movement, and clear physical form.

Key modern sighting clusters:

- **Rattlesnake Island**

- **Peachland shoreline**

- **Mission Bay**

- **Ellison Park region**

- **North of Kelowna near Bear Creek**

- **Naramata bench waters**

Some of the most credible witnesses include:

- RCMP officers

- Long-haul truckers

- Commercial divers

- Charter boat operators

- Lifeguards

- Biologists on research outings

And the descriptions match across decades:

- A **long, dark body**, often segmented

- **Humps rising and falling** in succession

- A head described as **horse-like** or **seal-like**

- Wake patterns suggesting a large, fast-moving entity

- Sudden dives with no bubbles and no debris

One of the most famous sightings occurred in **1968**, when a group of local residents filmed a series of humps moving rapidly across the lake.The video was studied extensively — and while inconclusive, the movement pattern didn't match any known large animal in the region.

A 1991 sighting by three witnesses described a **20–30 foot creature** following a boat before slipping beneath the surface.

In 2011, two families at a lakeside campground saw something large rise and submerge near the beach — close enough to cause a visible disturbance in the shallows.

In 2018, a drone operator captured a long, dark shape moving beneath the surface near the Naramata cliffs, disappearing into deeper water.

And every summer, new stories emerge — most from people who have never believed in monsters.

Sonar Hits: Evidence From the Deep

Okanagan Lake is **232 meters (760 feet)** deep.Most people don't realize how dark and cold it becomes just a few meters down.

Several major sonar hits have been recorded:

The 1980s Depth Scan

A charter boat's sonar picked up a **40-foot object** moving beneath the hull.It traveled faster than known large fish and maintained a consistent depth.

The 1991 Expedition

Professional sonar teams recorded a **solid, moving target** at approximately 60 feet that kept pace with the boat.

Experts who reviewed the data concluded the mass was significant enough to rule out fish or debris.

The 2018 Sonar Hit Near Rattlesnake Island

An angler's sonar recorded a long, uniform shape moving beneath his boat.The recording, analyzed by technicians, showed a target approximately **20–30 feet long**.

While none of these hits offer proof, they do one important thing:

They show something is down there, and it's big.

The Photographs — Sorting the Noise From the Signal

Hundreds of "Ogopogo photos" exist.Most are:

- waves

- wakes

- logs

- shadows

- floating debris

But a few stand out.

The 1970 "Row of Humps" Photo

Taken near Peachland, showing a clean series of dark humps moving in a line.This image has never been definitively explained.

The 1989 Peachland Photograph

A long, serpentine shape partially breaking the surface — clear enough that skeptics struggled to label it a log.

The 2000 Mission Bay Photograph

Two friends captured a large, dark object rising from the water around dusk.The scale suggests something **much larger than an otter or sturgeon.**

2020 Paddleboarder Photo

A paddleboarder near Kelowna shot a photo of a massive dark line beneath him — straight, uniform, and over 20 feet long.

Do photos prove anything?No.But they support something critical: **consistency**.

The same shapes.The same movement.The same locations.

For a century.

The Creature Theories — What Could Ogopogo Be?

People have tried to explain Ogopogo in many ways.

Here are the leading theories:

1. Sturgeon (Likely for some sightings, not for all)

- Okanagan Lake hosts sturgeon, but in low numbers.

- None documented reach the length or behavior described.

- Sturgeon do not create humps or wakes across the surface.

2. Eel or Unknown Fish Species

A large eel-like creature could explain some underwater shapes, but nothing known matches the size reported.

3. Surviving Plesiosaur (Popular but unlikely)

The cold water could support a large aquatic reptile, but the fossil record does not support modern survival.

4. Basilosaurus-type Mammal (More plausible)

A long, serpentine mammal similar to early whales could create visible humps and surface movement.

5. A Spiritual Phenomenon (Syilx perspective)

Some elders insist Ogopogo is not an animal — it is an entity.A guardian.Not meant to be captured or measured.

This theory aligns well with:

- sudden, unexplained storms

- disappearances

- sightings that appear and vanish instantly

- times when the lake seems to "wake up"

It might not be physical in the way we expect.

And perhaps that's the point.

Case Files — Ogopogo Encounters

Case File 11A — The Truck Driver's Encounter (1987)

A long-haul driver parked at a lakeside pullout saw a massive creature surface three times, each time creating a wake that rocked nearby boats.

Case File 11B — The Lifeguard Report (2003)

A lifeguard at a Kelowna beach saw something long and dark move beneath a group of swimmers about 30 meters offshore.No one was harmed — but the swimmers reported feeling a "cold rush" of water as it passed.

Case File 11C — The Drone Footage (2018)

A recreational drone operator captured a long, dark form passing beneath shallow water before descending into the depths.The footage shows a uniform, undulating shape.

Case File 11D — The Fisherman's Wake (2021)

Two anglers near Rattlesnake Island experienced a sudden, powerful wake with no boats nearby.Moments later, a dark shape surfaced briefly before sinking straight down.

Why Ogopogo Endures

The most compelling thing about Ogopogo isn't the photos or sonar.It's the continuity — **the unbroken chain of stories** from ancient Indigenous traditions to modern eyewitnesses.

People from all cultures, all backgrounds, all ages describe:

- the same shape

- the same movement

- the same locations

- the same unease, awe, and bewilderment

And Okanagan Lake itself feels like part of the mystery — deep, cold, quiet, and ancient.

This isn't a Nessie copycat.It isn't a tourist invention.It isn't a hoax blown out of proportion.

Long before the Okanagan Valley filled with orchards, vineyards, and summer homes, this lake was known as a place of power — a place with a guardian spirit.

And every time someone sees a series of dark humps sliding across the water, or a long shadow drifting beneath a boat, that spirit seems a little less like a legend and a little more like something still alive.

Something patient.Something watching.

CHAPTER 12 — CADBOROSAURUS: THE PACIFIC SERPENT
From Mud Bay to Haida Gwaii — The Creature That Keeps Returning

If Ogopogo is the inland monarch of BC's water mysteries, then **Cadborosaurus** is the coastal phantom — a creature that has haunted shores, fishing fleets, and Indigenous oral histories for centuries.Its territory is vast: the entire Pacific coastline from Puget Sound to Alaska.But its heartland — its true home — is British Columbia.

"Caddy," as many locals call it, is not a single-lake legend.This creature belongs to the ocean, the most unforgiving, unpredictable, and unexplored frontier on Earth. And unlike Ogopogo, whose identity is tied to one specific lake, Cadborosaurus is tied to **an entire coastline**, slipping between inlets, storm channels, kelp forests, and deep ocean canyons like a shadow.

The modern name may be charming.But the sightings are not.

Witnesses describe a creature that looks prehistoric — long, serpentine, powerful, often moving with a fluidity that no seal or whale can match. Something that breaks the surface in segments, like a creature with a body that coils beneath the waves.

It appears near beaches, in bays, around fishing boats, and sometimes alongside ferries.And every few decades, the coast erupts with a flurry of reports as if the animal migrates through in cycles.

For a century, and likely long before, the Pacific Northwest has whispered the same question:

What exactly is Cadborosaurus?

Origins: Before the Name, Before the Newspapers

Long before settlers arrived, coastal Indigenous Nations — including the Haida, Nuu-chah-nulth, Coast Salish, Kwakwaka'wakw, and Tlingit — told stories of **long-bodied sea beings** that hunted seals, traveled through channels, and occasionally came ashore.

These beings were not "monsters."They were **part of the living ocean**, as real as orcas or sea lions.

Descriptions varied, but common features included:

- **Long serpentine bodies**

- **Horse-like heads**

- **Large, dark eyes**

- **Undulating movement**

- **Back humps rising and falling in sequence**

- **Fins or flippers tucked close to the body**

Early anthropologists documented multiple accounts that match modern reports almost perfectly:

"A creature of the deep, long as a canoe, head like a seal but with a mane, fast as the tide." — *Kwakwaka'wakw oral history fragment, 1880s*

"A serpent that travels the coastline, surfacing only when hunting." — *Tlingit account, pre-1900*

To these communities, Caddy wasn't a curiosity.It was a **known animal**, rare but not supernatural — a creature with patterns, habits, and a presence woven into the coast's relationship with the ocean.

The First Modern Sightings (1900–1930)

As European settlement expanded, strange reports began appearing in newspapers.

1905 — Victoria, BC

A group of fishermen saw a large serpentine creature swimming south of Discovery Island.Described as:

- 40 feet long

- horse-like head

- several humps

1913 — Haro Strait

A man aboard a steamer witnessed a "sea serpent" pacing the vessel for several minutes before diving.

1924 — Comox Bay

Two men fishing observed a long creature rise from the water and "roll" several humps in a wave-like motion.

But the sighting that made Cadborosaurus famous — the one that cemented the name — happened in 1933.

1933 — The Cadboro Bay Sighting That Started It All

In the summer of 1933, locals in **Cadboro Bay** began reporting a strange animal surfacing offshore.It was seen by multiple witnesses over several weeks.

Descriptions included:

- long serpentine body

- vertical undulations

- a head resembling a horse or camel

- speed faster than a small motorboat

Newspapers coined the term **"Cadborosaurus"** — meaning **"lizard of Cadboro Bay."**

Reporters treated the story like a curiosity.But the sightings didn't stop.

That same year, a group of children on the beach watched a creature roll several dark humps as it passed close to shore.Their parents didn't believe them…until adults started reporting the same thing.

By the end of the summer, Cadborosaurus was a household name.

And the sightings only got stranger.

The 1937 "Caddy Carcass": The Case That Refuses to Die

If one event keeps the scientific community tied to Cadborosaurus, it's the famous 1937 carcass.

Two whalers aboard the vessel **Vivian M** near Queen Charlotte Sound killed a sperm whale and discovered a strange creature **inside its stomach** — partially swallowed, but intact enough to study.

They photographed the remains, noting:

- a long serpentine body

- flippers

- a narrow head

- vertebrae unlike known BC species

The carcass was brought to shore and shown to several experienced whalers.All said the same thing:

"We've never seen anything like that."

The remains were eventually lost, sparking decades of debate.But the **photographs survive**, and they do not match any known fish, eel, shark, or marine mammal.

To this day, marine biologists cannot agree on what the "Caddy carcass" actually was.

Some claim it was a malformed fetal baleen whale.Others argue the proportions are wrong — the neck too long, the body too slender, the flippers oddly shaped.

Even skeptical researchers admit:

Nothing perfectly fits the carcass.

Major Sightings: From Victoria to Haida Gwaii

Cadborosaurus is not tied to one bay or island.Sightings stretch across the coastline:

Northern BC / Haida Gwaii

- Fishermen see a long creature surfacing near salmon schools

- Large humps cutting through mist-covered waters

- A head rising vertically, watching boats

Central Coast / Bella Bella to Klemtu

- Carved into Indigenous art

- Described in stories as "the long one beneath the waves"

Vancouver Island

- Nanaimo Harbour: long body gliding under docks

- Sooke Basin: creature following a speedboat

- Campbell River: eerie nighttime breaches

Georgia Strait & Gulf Islands

- Ferries encountering massive wakes

- Kelp beds disturbed in unusual patterns

- Dark shapes pacing vessels

Victoria / Cadboro Bay

Still one of the hotspots.Residents routinely report:

- rolling humps

- serpentine movement

- sudden deep dives

These aren't drunken fishermen or fringe believers.Witnesses include:

- military personnel

- marine biologists

- commercial divers

- conservation officers

- ferry crew

Many describe the same motion:

A creature that moves like a snake…but with the power of a whale.

Descriptions — The Creature Profile

Across hundreds of sightings, the descriptions are remarkably consistent.

Head

- horse-like

- sometimes seal-like

- elongated snout

- large dark eyes

Neck

- long and flexible

- often protrudes vertically from the water

Body

- 30–70 feet

- several humps visible during surface travel

- dark green, grey, brown, or black

Movement

- undulating, rolling

- fast bursts of speed

- surface gliding followed by abrupt dives

Behavior

- often curious but avoids close contact

- frequently near salmon runs

- sometimes follows boats

A few reports describe it on land — usually briefly, sliding back into the ocean at speeds that seem impossible for a creature of its size.

Theories — What Could Cadborosaurus Be?

Unlike Ogopogo, whose identity is tied to a lake spirit, Cadborosaurus carries a stronger biological mystery.

1. A Surviving Plesiosaur

Popular but unlikely — though the neck/head descriptions fit disturbingly well.

2. A Giant Eel Species

Pacific eels do not reach the reported sizes, but deep-sea relatives could.

3. An Unknown Seal or Sea Lion

Not likely — the movement is too serpentine, the body too long.

4. A Basilosaurus-Type Marine Mammal

This is the theory most cryptozoologists support:

- long serpentine body

- mammalian behavior

- evolved for cold waters

5. Misidentified Whale Calves

Possible for some sightings — but not for the ones involving slender bodies and humps.

6. A Reptile-Like Marine Predator

A new species entirely — something that evolved alongside whales and dolphins but avoided detection.

Case Files — Cadborosaurus Encounters

Case File 12A — The Military Report (1950)

A Royal Canadian Navy crew spotted a 60-foot creature pacing their vessel for nearly 10 minutes before diving deep.

Case File 12B — The Vancouver Harbour Incident (1998)

Dock workers saw a long serpentine shape slide between pilings, disturbing fish and seals.

Case File 12C — The Haida Gwaii Channel Sighting (2009)

Fishermen saw a dark, 40-foot creature rise twice, roll three humps, and disappear.

Case File 12D — The Ferry Encounter (2016)

BC Ferries crew reported a massive, unexplained wake crossing their bow with no boats nearby. Several passengers observed a long dark object surfacing briefly.

Why Cadborosaurus Endures

Unlike lake monsters confined to small watersheds, Cadborosaurus lives in an ocean so vast and unmapped it could easily hide an unknown species.

Every few years, new sightings remind the coast that something is still out there:

- long, rolling humps

- a horse-like head

- a serpentine body slicing the waves

The Pacific Northwest is full of mysteries — but few feel as real, as persistent, or as eerily plausible as Cadborosaurus.

Because here, in these deep channels and dark coastal inlets, the ocean is still wild enough to keep its secrets.

And every time a fisherman sees something rise from the mist, or a ferry passenger glimpses a shape under the waves, the legend breathes again.

Not as a myth.

But as a creature that may still be swimming just beneath the surface.

CHAPTER 13 — OTHER LAKE MYSTERIES OF BRITISH COLUMBIA
The Silent Waters Where Legends Linger

British Columbia is a province dominated by water — glacial lakes, mountain tarns, fjords, river-fed basins, volcanic bowls, and drowned valleys. Ogopogo may hold the crown, and Cadborosaurus commands the coastline, but they are far from the only aquatic mysteries lurking in BC.

Across the interior, locals whisper about **shadowy shapes beneath alpine lakes**, strange wakes that appear on windless mornings, gigantic forms passing beneath fishing boats, and animals no one can identify rising briefly before slipping back into deep, cold darkness.

Some of these stories date back hundreds of years.Some were recorded by early settlers.Others come from hikers, fishermen, forestry workers, and campers just in the last few decades.

Individually, they seem like isolated oddities — but when you map them across the province, a pattern begins to form.Not of a single species, but of **multiple distinct creatures**, tied to the unique ecological niches of BC's great lakes.

This chapter explores the "secondary mysteries" — the lesser-known but deeply fascinating lake legends from across the province.They don't have the fame of Ogopogo, and they don't have the oceanic range of Cadborosaurus.

But in some ways, they feel more visceral, more intimate — because their mysteries remain uncommercialized, almost untouched.

These lakes hold their secrets quietly.And the people who encounter their creatures never seem to forget.

SHUSWAP LAKE — The Long Black Shape of Copper Island

Shuswap Lake is a sprawling, branching body of water with depths exceeding 500 feet. It is one of the warmest major lakes in BC — perfect habitat for large fish, but also for something stranger.

For decades, boaters have reported:

- a **sleek, black form**, often 20–25 feet long

- a **submarine-like shadow** moving beneath clear water

- long wakes appearing on still mornings

- a creature traveling in **smooth, rolling arcs**, not splashing like a fish

One of the most persistent hotspots is around **Copper Island** near Blind Bay.Fishermen here routinely speak of a "big, dark something" that moves with intelligence.

In 1984, two men trolling for trout reported a long black shape pacing their boat, staying parallel with them for nearly 90 seconds.One said:

"It moved like a mammal. Smooth, deliberate. No thrashing, no tail splash. It was like watching a shadow with intent."

Divers have also reported uncomfortable encounters with something large moving beneath them — always out of view, but unmistakably present.

While officially unexplained, wildlife biologists admit the sightings **don't match sturgeon** or any known fish species in the lake.

WILLISTON LAKE — The Giant of the North

Williston Lake — BC's largest reservoir — is a drowned landscape of former mountains, valleys, and old-growth forest. Beneath its dark surface lies a world of timeless, untouched terrain.

Since the lake's creation in the 1960s, residents and boaters have described:

- long, serpentine bodies surfacing at dusk

- huge wakes traveling against the wind

- a creature with **multiple humps** traveling at surprising speed

- a head described as "seal-like but wrong"

One of the most credible reports comes from 1999, when a forestry crew on a barge platform witnessed a **30–40 foot creature** rise briefly, roll two massive humps, and disappear.

Another encounter, in 2007, involved a group of hunters crossing the lake at dawn. They saw something large enough to displace water like a small boat:

"It didn't behave like a fish. It behaved like something that knew we were watching."

Given the lake's vastness and limited access, many believe an unknown species — possibly related to the ocean-going Cadborosaurus — became trapped inland when the reservoir formed.

ATLIN LAKE — The Creature of the North Wind

Atlin Lake is one of the most remote and beautiful lakes in BC, often called "The Switzerland of the North." Its waters are deep, frigid, and surrounded by mountains that feel ancient.

Indigenous stories from the Taku River Tlingit describe a **long-bodied creature** inhabiting the lake, surfacing only when disturbed.

Settlers reported similar encounters in the 1930s and 1950s:

- a **serpentine creature**, 20–30 feet long

- dark body rising and falling in segments

- rapid dives into deep water

The most famous sighting occurred in 1975 when a local pilot, landing his floatplane, saw a large creature moving beneath the surface — long enough to stretch "half the length of a dock."

He later said:

"It was alive, moving with purpose, and bigger than anything I've ever seen in freshwater."

To this day, locals still speak cautiously of "the Atlin serpent."

HARRISON LAKE — Not Just a Sasquatch Valley

Harrison is famous for Sasquatch sightings — but the lake itself holds a parallel mystery.

Multiple witnesses over 60 years have described:

- long, dark bodies breaking the surface

- wakes with **no boat source**

- animal-like shapes pacing kayaks

- several-hump sequences moving near the shoreline

In 1968, a fishing guide reported watching a creature surface three times near Echo Island:

"If it was a fish, it was bigger than my boat. The humps were too perfect, spaced too evenly."

Given its proximity to the ocean — the Harrison River and Fraser River systems are linked — some believe **Cadborosaurus** may occasionally enter the lake.

Theories include:

- following salmon

- entering during high-water spring runoff

- using the inlet as a temporary hunting ground

If true, Harrison Lake may be one of the few places where BC's forest mysteries and water mysteries overlap.

KATHLYN LAKE — The Monster Nobody Talks About

Near Smithers, Kathlyn Lake is a quiet, unassuming mountain lake.No tourist brochures. No monster statues. No official legends.

But locals know the whispers.

Over the years they've reported:

- a massive shape moving beneath ice

- dark bodies cruising beneath boats

- something rising vertically, watching, then submerging

- unexplained nighttime ripples

- large wakes with no wind

One winter, a family ice fishing saw a long shadow pass **under the ice hole**, slow and deliberate. It was so large that the child thought it was "a log drifting underwater."

The father, shaken, said later:

"Logs don't change direction."

SKELETON LAKE — The Northern Unknown

Not to be confused with the Ontario lake of the same name, BC's Skeleton Lake lies east of Fort Nelson in a remote stretch of boreal wilderness.

There are only a handful of known reports, but each is striking:

- a creature with a dark, eel-like body

- massive wakes on still water

- a head described as "seal but stretched"

A 2002 report from a trapper described a 20-foot creature rising near his canoe, its head turning toward him before it vanished beneath the water with a smooth, powerful dive.

"It wasn't frightened. It was just curious. But I've never paddled away so quietly in my life."

LESSER-KNOWN LAKE CREATURES OF BC

Scattered across the province are dozens of one-off sightings and localized legends. Some are likely misidentifications — but others feel stranger.

Cultus Lake

Sightings of a "dark swimmer" with a long body.

Ootsa Lake

Reports of massive wakes and dark underwater silhouettes.

Quesnel Lake

One fisherman described a creature "rolling humps like a dolphin but far too long."

Muncho Lake

Tourists have reported a shadow following boats for hundreds of meters.

Gwillim Lake

A biologist saw an object "the size of a minivan" move beneath his canoe.

Indigenous stories frequently refer to **water guardians** or **lake protectors** in these regions — some benevolent, some territorial.

THEORY: DIFFERENT CREATURES, OR ONE TYPE ADAPTING?

Looking across BC's lakes, three possibilities emerge:

1. Multiple Species

Freshwater serpents, giant eels, mammalian predators — each confined to its own lake or region.

2. One Species With a Wide Range

Perhaps a freshwater/estuarine version of Cadborosaurus capable of moving between river systems.

3. A Spirit/Guardian Phenomenon

Indigenous knowledge suggests some of these beings are **not animals**, but territorial forces tied to specific waters.

This theory explains:

- sudden vanishings

- seasonal appearances

- lakes that seem "alive"

- encounters that feel more intuitive than physical

Not every report must be biological.Sometimes the land is trying to tell a story we no longer know how to hear.

CASE FILES — OTHER LAKE CREATURES

Case File 13A — Shuswap Shadow (1996)

Two boaters see a long black shape pacing them in 40 feet of water.

Case File 13B — Williston Wake (2007)

Hunters witness massive humps rolling across the lake at dawn.

Case File 13C — Atlin Depth Encounter (1975)

Floatplane pilot sees large creature beneath the surface upon landing.

Case File 13D — Harrison Lake Triple-Surface (1968)

A fishing guide watches three humps surface in sequence near Echo Island.

Case File 13E — Kathlyn Under-Ice Shadow (2001)

Family ice fishing sees a large shape pass beneath the hole.

Why These Lakes Matter

BC's little-known lake mysteries aren't sideshows to Ogopogo.They're evidence of a broader, deeper pattern:

- **unknown aquatic animals**

- **ancient Indigenous knowledge**

- **consistent reports** over decades

- **isolated lakes capable of hiding large species**

This province is old, vast, and largely unexplored underwater.

And in these quiet lakes, away from the spotlight, the water still moves in ways that defy explanation.

Not every mystery demands fame.Some prefer the silence.

CHAPTER 14 — MISSING IN THE MOUNTAINS

The Garibaldi Triangle, North Shore Vanishings & the Dead Zones of the Coast Range

British Columbia is a province defined by mountains — sharp, angular, ice-carved teeth rising straight from the sea, stacked behind one another like an endless wall. Tourists see postcard beauty. Locals see home. But anyone who has spent real time in these ranges knows something else entirely:

People disappear here. Not occasionally.Not rarely.But consistently — in ways that defy normal explanation.

You can blame terrain, weather, misadventure, hypothermia, and predators. All of those things claim lives every year. Yet some cases — the stubborn handful that live in Search and Rescue memory for decades — don't fit the checklist.

Tracks that stop.Trails that end.Victims found in places they shouldn't be.Or never found at all.

This chapter explores the **Garibaldi Triangle**, the **Vancouver North Shore vanishings**, and the broader **Coast Range dead zones** — a cluster of disappearances so strange, so patterned, that even experienced SAR veterans shake their heads when they talk about them.

This isn't sensationalism.This is a pattern — one that stretches back more than a century.

THE GARIBALDI TRIANGLE

A Region Where People Walk Into the Trees and Do Not Walk Out

The Garibaldi region — roughly bordered by Squamish, Whistler, and Pemberton — is a place of raw, vertical wilderness. Deep glaciated valleys, volcanic ridgelines, towering peaks, storms that appear out of nowhere, and forests so dense that a person can vanish from sight in seconds.

SAR teams know it well.And they know its reputation.

The Disappearance Zone

Roughly speaking, the Garibaldi Triangle includes:

- Garibaldi Lake

- Black Tusk

- Rubble Creek

- Cheakamus Lake

- Wedgemount

- Singing Pass

- The upper Green River basin

It's enormous.It's hostile.And for decades, it has produced disappearances with a disturbing level of mystery.

The 1963 Five Students — Garibaldi Lake

One of the most enduring mysteries in BC history involves **five Vancouver students** who vanished while attempting to climb a ridge near Garibaldi Lake in the winter of 1963.

Search teams found:

- no bodies

- no equipment

- no sign of a fall

- no avalanche debris

- no tracks leading away

Their footprints simply **stopped** on a ridgeline.

After weeks of searching, the official conclusion was "presumed buried by avalanche," but every SAR member present knew the truth — there was **no avalanche field** in the area they vanished.

To this day, there are no answers.

The 1997 Black Tusk Trail Runner

A trained mountain runner vanished near Black Tusk while on a solo day run.He signed the trail register.People saw him jogging uphill that morning.But somewhere between Taylor Meadows and the lower switchbacks, he vanished.

Search teams found:

- a single footprint

- then nothing

- no pack

- no clothing

- no body

This is a trail with limited side paths and steady foot traffic.He was never seen again.

The 2004 Cheakamus Lake Camper

A man camping alone near Cheakamus Lake left his tent to get water — he told this to a neighbouring camper — and simply never returned.

His tent remained zipped open.His shoes were found near the shoreline.His tracks led to the water......and then **stopped** at the edge.

RCMP divers found no body.No clothing.No disturbance on the lakebed.

One SAR member later admitted:

"It's like he was lifted out of the world."

THE NORTH SHORE VANISHINGS

One of the Densest Clusters of Missing People in Canada

The North Shore Mountains rise directly behind one of the largest cities in Canada — Vancouver. On clear days they look welcoming, almost gentle. But anyone who's spent time in Lynn Headwaters, Seymour, Grouse, or Cypress knows the truth:

The North Shore eats people.

Not metaphorically — statistically.

Lynn Headwaters alone has had **over 40 disappearances** in modern records, many permanently unsolved.

This region includes:

- Lynn Valley

- Lynn Headwaters

- Hanes Valley

- Mount Seymour

- Mount Fromme

- Grouse Mountain

- Capilano watershed

These are not remote wilderness areas — some are only minutes from city limits. And yet the disappearances here rival those of the Yukon and Alaska when scaled by area.

The 1993 Tom Thiessen Case — A Vanishing Point

Thiessen began a solo hike in Lynn Headwaters.He signed the logbook.He was experienced, well-equipped, and familiar with the area.

He was never found.

Not a pack.Not a shoe.Not a scrap of clothing.

Searchers later pointed out something unusual — the **search dogs acted strangely**, circling in confused loops, then refusing to continue upslope in a certain ravine.

One handler said:

"It was like the forest went silent. No birds. Nothing. The dog didn't want to go in."

Mount Seymour — The Trail That Isn't Safe

Multiple disappearances have occurred around Dog Mountain, Third Peak, and the Mystery Lake region. Some of the strangest include:

The 1989 Snowshoe Hiker

A man was seen near First Peak.He waved to another hiker.Minutes later — gone.

Search teams found:

- a single snowshoe track

- then nothing

- no sign of a slide

- no prints beyond a few meters

The 2014 Trail Runner

A well-conditioned runner vanished on the Baden-Powell Trail.He left his car at the trailhead.His GPS watch was later found on the trail — stopped abruptly mid-log.

He was never located.

HANES VALLEY — THE DEAD PASSAGE

Hanes Valley is considered one of the most dangerous wilderness corridors on the North Shore. Not because of cliffs or weather — though those are bad enough — but because **people go missing here at an alarming rate**.

SAR members speak quietly about:

- strange echo patterns

- "wrong sound" forests

- sudden silences

- weather that shifts unnaturally quickly

- people reporting being watched or shadowed on the trail

One SAR member, interviewed anonymously, said:

"Hanes Valley has places where sound dies. If you yell, it just… stops. You feel it in your stomach."

COAST RANGE DEAD ZONES

Areas SAR Teams Quietly Acknowledge as Problematic

These aren't marked on maps. You won't find them in guidebooks. But SAR teams across BC recognize "dead zones" — regions with:

- unusual disappearance patterns

- navigation anomalies

- strange echo or silence patterns

- disorientation zones

- abrupt emotional reactions from hikers

- compasses acting strangely

These areas include:

- The upper Pitt River drainage

- The backcountry between Squamish and the Elaho

- Pemberton Icecap margins

- Remote Hanes Valley side basins

- Hidden basins east of Mount Seymour

- Upper Cheakamus canyon plateaus

Most hikers never experience anything unusual.But those who do rarely forget it.

THEORIES — WHAT'S REALLY HAPPENING?

Search and Rescue explains most vanishings with:

- terrain hazards

- hypothermia

- predator encounters

- disorientation

- falls

- water hazards

But even SAR leaders admit some cases remain "fundamentally inexplicable."

Here are the working theories:

1. Terrain Swallowing People

BC mountains contain:

- deep crevasses

- rotted-out snow bridges

- limestone sinkholes

- hidden ravines

- deadfall pits

A body falling into one of these features may never be found.

2. Sudden Weather Shifts

The Coast Range is notorious for cloud inversions and sudden storms.Visibility can drop to zero in minutes.People walk off trails without realizing it.

3. Human Error Compounded by Terrain

In BC, one wrong step can mean:

- falling into a canyon

- sliding into timber

- hitting a tree well

- entering a gully too steep to climb

Many vanishings likely occurred this way — but the **lack of remains** is still troubling.

4. Animal Predation

Cougars and bears are common, but they **rarely fully consume remains**.Most SAR cases show signs of predation — these strange ones do not.

5. Something Else

This category is rarely spoken aloud.

But the truth is:British Columbia has vanishings that feel... off.

- footprints ending on bare rock

- dogs refusing to enter certain areas

- GPS devices failing

- radio transmissions cutting out

- hikers reporting "feeling pulled" off trail

- sudden dread in specific spots

Some SAR members privately believe the land itself plays a role — not supernatural, but **something old**, an environmental or psychological force we do not yet understand.

CASE FILES — MISSING IN THE MOUNTAINS

Case File 14A — The Lynn Headwaters Triangulation (2008)

Three hikers vanished in separate incidents within 1 kilometre of each other — over a 14-year span. None were found.

Case File 14B — The Whistler Disappearing Tracks (1999)

Runner's tracks stopped mid-trail.No slide.No snow disturbance.

Case File 14C — The Seymour Single Print (1989)

One snowshoe track found.Then nothing.Search teams still talk about it.

THE REALITY OF VANISHING

Not all disappearances are mysterious.But enough *are* that they form a pattern — a quiet one, spoken mostly among SAR veterans and wilderness guides.

Something in these mountains takes people.Not maliciously.Not intentionally.

But powerfully.Silently.Completely.

The Coast Range is beautiful — but it's a beauty that demands humility.

The moment you believe you're safe is the moment you stop noticing the small signs that the mountain is shifting around you.

And some people never realize that shift until it's too late.

CHAPTER 15 — THE HIGHWAY 16 MYSTERY

Vanishings Along the Highway of Tears & the Wilderness That Remembers

There are places in British Columbia where the land feels heavy — where silence hangs over the forests in a way you can't quite explain, and where the wind seems to carry stories that never made it to the newspapers.Highway 16, stretching across the northern spine of the province from Prince Rupert to Prince George, is one of those places.

To many Canadians, it's known as the **Highway of Tears** — a corridor of disappearances, unsolved cases, violent incidents, and families left without answers. The name itself is loaded with grief, injustice, and generations of pain. But behind the headlines and political discussions lies something deeper, older, and harder to define:

This region has always been a place where people disappear. Long before Highway 16 existed.Long before communities were built along its length.Long before the road connected the coast to the interior.

The rivers, the forests, the steep valleys, the endless plateaus — they have swallowed people for centuries.

This chapter is not about the criminal investigations, which are well known and heavily documented elsewhere.This chapter is about the *geography*, the *patterns*, the *oddities*, and the purely wilderness-related vanishings and strange events that occur along the same corridor.

The human tragedies are real.The wild mysteries are real.And in this rare place, they overlap in ways that make even seasoned Search and Rescue workers uneasy.

THE CORRIDOR OF DISAPPEARANCE

A Land Shaped by Rivers, Storms, and Shadowed Forest

From Prince Rupert to Terrace, the highway winds along the Skeena River — a broad, fast-moving waterway with steep cliffs and dense cedar forests. Farther east, the landscape opens into rolling valleys, wetlands, and boreal forest. Then the road rises into plateaus, drifts through endless timber, passes through tiny towns, and cuts across rivers that have drowned entire logging crews.

The wilderness here is not decorative.It is absolute.

People vanish in places where help is hours — sometimes days — away. Cellular reception is patchy. Weather shifts in minutes. And the forest is thick, silent, and difficult to navigate even in daylight.

For many disappearances, terrain alone could explain the loss.But others?Others defy the logic of experienced search teams.

THE ANCIENT PATTERN — BEFORE HIGHWAY 16 EXISTED

Indigenous Nations living along this corridor — Gitxsan, Wet'suwet'en, Carrier Sekani, and several others — have stories going back long before colonial settlement of:

- travelers disappearing without a trace

- forest spirits that lure individuals off trails

- sudden disorientation in specific valleys

- beings that stalk the tree line

- rivers that "take" people

- mountains that "don't give back"

These are not myths told to frighten children.They are warnings — cultural memory wrapped in story form.

For generations, the elders said the same thing:

"There are parts of these lands that humans should not enter alone."

And when you look at the modern patterns, it becomes impossible to ignore just how accurate those warnings were.

BRITISH COLUMBIA SAR — THE CASES THAT DON'T ADD UP

Search and Rescue workers along Highway 16 deal with missing-person calls every year — hikers, hunters, berry pickers, mushroom foragers, travelers who stepped off the shoulder of the highway and into the treeline.

Most are found.

But the ones that aren't?Those cases form a pattern that gives SAR veterans the same uneasy look as the North Shore cases down south.

Characteristics of the unsolved wilderness disappearances include:

- **footprints ending abruptly**

- **search dogs losing all scent at specific spots**

- **victims found far from their expected route**

- **weather anomalies during disappearances**

- **areas with sudden, unnatural silence**

- **extremely rapid onset of disorientation**

- **cases where the missing were only minutes ahead of rescuers — yet vanished**

And these cases often cluster in the exact same places, decade after decade.

This is the Highway 16 mystery most people have never heard of.

THE SKEENA RIVER SECTION

A Waterway That Takes Without Warning

The section between **Prince Rupert and Terrace** is one of the wildest stretches of highway in Canada. The Skeena River surges beside the road — cold, fast, relentless, capable of swallowing a person and not returning them for months, if ever.

Some disappearances here can be explained by the river alone.Others cannot.

The 1978 Angler Disappearance

A fisherman went missing near Usk. His footprints led to the riverbank — then continued **onto a gravel bar that did not exist at low tide**. His pack was found intact. No slide. No signs of a fall.He was never recovered.

The Terrace Shadows Case (1992)

Two loggers driving at dusk saw a figure standing on the shoulder. They slowed, thinking it was a hitchhiker — but the figure stepped into the treeline. The men stopped, concerned, and shone their headlights into the brush.

Nothing.No tracks.No broken branches.Fresh snow — undisturbed.

They later learned someone had gone missing in that exact area days earlier.

THE BULKLEY VALLEY PATTERN

Smithers, Houston, Telkwa — Places of Sudden Vanishings

This valley is full of hunters, hikers, and families who know the land well. But it is also home to a string of disappearances with unsettling similarities.

The 1986 Houston Search

A local hunter vanished less than 400 meters from a forestry road. SAR teams found:

- clear boot tracks

- then a sudden stop

- no sign of struggle

- no predation

- no avalanche

His rifle was later found leaning against a tree, carefully placed.

The man was not.

The Smithers Ridge Case (2004)

A man hiking on a clear fall afternoon saw someone waving to him from a ridge ahead. He waved back, climbed toward the figure — and found no one. No prints. No sign of descent. The ridge dead-ended at a cliff.

He turned back shortly after. SAR received a call later that day: a young woman had gone missing in the same area.

THE WET'SUWET'EN TERRITORY WILDERNESS ZONES

Certain areas near Burns Lake and Fraser Lake have long been considered dangerous, especially alone or at dusk.

Elders speak of:

- **forest beings** that mimic voices

- places where "the trees move differently"

- **dead pockets of air** where sound disappears

- lakes that "take people under"

- valleys where hunters lose hours of memory

These experiences mirror modern SAR reports with uncanny precision.

THE HIGHWAY ITSELF — WHERE PEOPLE STEP OFF AND VANISH

Multiple highway-adjacent disappearances have occurred within **30 metres of the road**, often in broad daylight.

Case: The 1999 Rest-Stop Vanishing

A man pulled over near Topley for a washroom break.His partner watched him walk toward the treeline.He never came back.

RCMP found:

- no tracks

- no clothing

- no personal items

- no body

The forest floor was mossy and soft — tracks should have been obvious.There were none.

Case: The 2011 Shoulder Stop

A vehicle broke down near Hagwilget.A man walked 15 metres into the brush to relieve himself.

Gone.

A full search — dogs, grid teams, river checks, drones, helicopters — found nothing.

THEORIES — WHAT IS REALLY HAPPENING ALONG HIGHWAY 16?

No single explanation covers all cases. But the vanishings fall into categories that SAR members quietly acknowledge.

1. Dangerous Terrain

Some areas are riddled with:

- sudden drop-offs

- unstable ground

- deep bogs

- hidden creeks

- sinkholes

- animal dens

- river undercuts

A fall into one of these features can make a recovery impossible.

2. Rivers That Take and Never Return

The Skeena, Bulkley, Babine, and Nass Rivers are cold, violent, and unpredictable. Many bodies are never recovered.

3. Hypothermia + Disorientation

Even experienced hikers can become disoriented in BC's dense forests, especially when weather shifts rapidly.

4. Wildlife — Rare, But Possible

Bears and cougars do kill people, but again — **they do not erase footprints or leave no evidence**.

5. Human Danger

Along Highway 16, human-caused disappearances are undeniably part of the picture.But they do not account for:

- footprints stopping mid-trail

- vanishings in remote, inaccessible wilderness

- cases where no trace is ever found despite massive searches

These belong to a different category entirely.

6. The Land Itself

This is the part few talk about openly.

Some SAR teams, Indigenous elders, and long-time locals believe certain parts of this land have a presence — not supernatural, but *ancient*:

- geological anomalies that disturb navigation

- infrasound from wind corridors

- magnetic disturbances

- environmental psychological effects

- places where you become disoriented instantly

Others believe it's something older:

"There are places you respect because the land remembers.If you don't listen, it takes you back."— Gitxsan Elder, 1980s

CASE FILES — HIGHWAY 16 WILDERNESS VANISHINGS

Case File 15A — The Skeena Footprint Stop (1978)

Footprints lead onto a temporary gravel bar.The man vanishes.Never seen again.

Case File 15B — Houston Rifle Tree (1986)

Hunter's rifle left neatly against a tree.Him — gone without trace.

Case File 15C — Topley Rest-Stop Vanishing (1999)

Man walks into brush.Never exits.No tracks.

Case File 15D — Hagwilget Shoulder Mystery (2011)

Man steps off road.Disappears in seconds.

WHY HIGHWAY 16 HAUNTS US

There is no single explanation.No single killer.No single cause.

Instead, Highway 16 is a place where:

- wilderness
- weather
- rivers
- history
- human vulnerability
- Indigenous memory

- forgotten tragedies

- and patterns we don't yet understand

all collide.

People vanish here because the land is vast and unforgiving.Others vanish for reasons no SAR team can explain.And some vanish in ways that feel like the past reaching out through the trees.

Highway 16 is not cursed.It is simply alive — and far older than the road we built across its spine.

CHAPTER 16 — SEARCH & RESCUE: CASES THAT DEFY LOGIC
When the Mountain Gives No Answers

Search & Rescue teams in British Columbia are some of the most skilled in the world. They have to be — this province demands it. Between the glacier-cut mountains, unstable cliffs, sudden storms, deep coastal rainforests, and endless plateaus of timber, SAR members operate in terrain that can overwhelm even experienced mountaineers.

Most missions end the way you expect:someone got turned around, slipped off a trail, underestimated a storm, or followed an animal track instead of a human path. These rescues make sense. They follow patterns. They fit.

But every SAR group in BC — North Shore Rescue, Squamish, Coquitlam, Prince George, Terrace, Smithers, Pemberton, Golden — has stories they don't put in public reports.

Cases that make no sense.Cases that defy their training.Cases that don't follow the rules of terrain, weather, or human behavior.

Some call them "the weird ones."Others call them "black files."Most SAR members just refer to them as:

"The cases we don't talk about unless you've been there."

This chapter collects those rare stories — the ones SAR veterans still remember years later, the ones they revisit in late-night conversations when the radios are quiet and the campfire is burning low.

These are not supernatural tales.They are cases where the logic breaks down — the map doesn't add up, the footprints don't align with physics, the forest goes silent when it shouldn't, and the missing person acts in ways no survival instructor can explain.

THE SILENCE ZONES

"It's like the forest turns off."

SAR teams repeatedly describe areas where the sound dies completely —
not gradually, but instantly, like someone flipped a switch.

These zones appear in:

- Hanes Valley

- Seymour back basins

- Upper Pitt drainage

- Hidden creeks off Howe Sound

- Deep sections of the Telkwa range

- The Elaho-Pemberton divide

- Certain side gullies near Garibaldi Lake

A veteran of North Shore Rescue explained it like this:

"You could be in normal forest one second — birds, wind, everything —
and then step ten feet forward and it goes dead. No sound. No echo. The
radio crackles. The dog gets nervous. You don't stay there long."

These dead-sound pockets consistently overlap with **disappearance
clusters**.

SAR dogs often:

- refuse to enter

- lose all scent

- whine or growl

- circle in confusion

It's not every search.Not every forest.Not even most of them.

But when it happens, the team notes it — quietly.

THE "WRONG-SHAPE" FORESTS

Trails that bend, landmarks that move, and distances that feel incorrect

Several SAR members from Squamish and Pemberton have reported instances where:

- distances felt longer or shorter than normal

- compass bearings shifted by several degrees

- trails seemed to bend in ways they never had before

- landmarks appeared "off," slightly relocated

- batteries drained more quickly than expected

These aren't hallucinations — multiple team members experience them at the same time.

One SAR member described a search near the Ashlu area:

"We walked up a ridge and it didn't match the map. The river sounded farther away than it should. And when we came back down, the same section of forest looked different. We took photos and compared them. Nothing wrong with the forest. Something wrong with us."

These cases tend to happen in areas with steep granite columns or ancient landslide fields — places where magnetic interference is plausible…but not fully explanatory.

DISAPPEARING TRACKS

Footprints that should continue, but don't

SAR teams expect to follow a missing person's tracks until:

- terrain shifts

- snow blows over

- vegetation changes

- a river interrupts the trail

But in certain BC cases, the tracks end for no reason.

Case: The Black Tusk Runner (1999)

Tracks led clearly along a trail.Then stopped in the middle of a straight path.No wind.No ice.No debris.No slide.

Case: The Telkwa Ridge Hiker (2007)

Bootprints led to a clearing of soft moss — ideal for catching impressions.But after one clean print, the ground showed nothing for twenty metres.He was never found.

Case: The Coquitlam Trail Walker (2013)

Dog-scent was strong for 500 metres, then vanished abruptly at a mossy boulder field.

These cases haunt SAR members more than anything else.Tracks tell stories.When they stop telling stories, something is wrong.

THE "OUT-OF-PLACE" FINDS

Clothing, shoes, and gear found where they shouldn't be

Searchers frequently discover strange patterns of discarded clothing during hypothermia cases — known as paradoxical undressing.

But some finds do not fit hypothermia, trauma, or panic.

Case: The Seymour Shoe Ridge (2015)

A missing hiker's shoe was found on a ridge they could not physically have reached without ropes. The shoe was sitting upright, as if placed deliberately.

Case: The Skeena Jacket Fold (2002)

A jacket belonging to a missing angler was found neatly folded under a tree root in a location he would never have walked to — a steep, slippery drainage.

Case: The Whistler Watch Placement (2008)

A fitness watch belonging to a trail runner was found on a stump, unharmed, with GPS history showing no signs of distress. The runner vanished without trace.

SAR reports note these items as "found," but they rarely comment on the strangeness.

THE SURVIVOR STORIES — PEOPLE WHO CAME BACK

These are rare, but they matter — because sometimes the missing do return, and what they say often matches SAR's unspoken concerns.

Survivor: The Pemberton Bushwalker (2011)

A man went missing for 36 hours.When found, he said:

"The forest felt wrong. I couldn't hear birds. I kept walking but the forest didn't feel like it was moving with me. I don't know how else to describe it."

Survivor: The Seymour Disorientation Case (2019)

A hiker wandered only 500 metres off trail — but lost all sense of direction.

He said:

"I walked toward the sound of the creek. Then it sounded behind me. Then it sounded above me. None of it made sense."

This matches dozens of SAR experiences in disorientation zones.

Survivor: The Elaho Watcher (2006)

A hunter spent a night lost in a valley near the Elaho River.

He claimed:

"Something walked around me all night. Two legs. Slow. It didn't come closer. But it didn't leave."

SAR does not comment on this.But they privately confirmed the man was physically healthy and not hypothermic.

THEORIES SAR MEMBERS DISCUSS QUIETLY

No SAR team endorses supernatural explanations.But many acknowledge the unknown.

Here are the theories that circulate:

1. Magnetic or Geological Anomalies

Granite spires, iron deposits, and fault lines may disturb:

- compass readings

- GPS signals

- dog tracking

- human orientation

This is the most accepted theory — but does not explain disappearing tracks.

2. Infrasound

Low-frequency sound waves can cause:

- panic

- nausea

- disorientation

- auditory hallucinations

- tunnel vision

Wind channels in the Coast Range may create infrasound pockets.

3. Predator Behavior

Bears and cougars may drag bodies away — but they do not erase footprints or clothing.

4. Terrain That "Eats People"

BC has:

- lava tubes

- deep fissures

- hidden crevasses

- moss-covered holes

- river undercuts

A fall into one of these features can be unrecoverable.

5. Something Ancient In the Landscape

This is said quietly, with caution.

Some SAR veterans — and many Indigenous elders — believe the land itself has places where humans are not meant to be.

Not malevolent.Not sentient in the human sense.

But resonant.

As one SAR member put it:

"There are places you can walk into, but you might not walk out."

CASE FILES — THE SEARCHES THAT STILL HAUNT THEM

Case File 16A — The Elaho Missing Camper

The man's tent was zipped.Food untouched.Boots inside.He stepped out
barefoot — and vanished.

Case File 16B — The Grouse Grid Search

Searchers combed one area six times.On the seventh, they found the
missing man's hat sitting in the middle of a clearing they had walked
through repeatedly.

Case File 16C — The Pitt Lake Echo Case

A father and son separated by only 20 metres.The father turned his head
— and the child was gone.No tracks.Hours later, the boy was found
unharmed but confused, claiming he had walked "into the quiet place."

THE TRUTH SAR LEARN THE HARD WAY

Search and Rescue teams don't fear the wilderness.They respect it.

They know the rules:

- the mountain wins

- the weather decides

- the forest hides more than it reveals

- the river will not negotiate

- the dark comes faster up here

- and the missing do not always want to be found

But the strangest lesson — the one whispered around base camps — is this:

Some parts of BC want you gone.Some parts want you to leave.And some parts simply do not give you back.

CHAPTER 17 — GHOST TOWNS OF THE NORTH
Echoes in Abandoned Valleys

British Columbia is full of places that look alive on the map but are dead in the real world.

Names that once meant something — towns with churches, sawmills, schools, general stores, saloons, bunkhouses, and families — now reduced to rotting foundations swallowed by alder roots. If you stand in these places long enough, the only thing reminding you they ever existed is the way the ground feels slightly unnatural under your boots. Flattened by human hands generations ago, then reclaimed grain by grain by the forest.

Most people drive past these ghost towns without knowing they're there. Others seek them out of curiosity. And then there are those who feel something deeper when they step into a forgotten valley — a strange pressure in the air, a sense that someone is standing just out of sight, watching from where the mill floor used to be.

This chapter isn't about ghost stories in the traditional sense — though BC has plenty of those. It's about *places* that don't seem empty, even when they are. Places where history doesn't settle. Places where the ground holds memory like damp soil holds the cold.

Ghost towns in British Columbia are not silent.Not really.

THE LOST MINING TOWNS OF THE KOOTENAYS

Where the Mountains Remember Every Life Spent in Them

The Kootenays are stitched together by mining towns that rose and fell so fast their stories barely had time to breathe. Today, if you hike through Sandon or cross the creek into the remains of Cody, you can almost hear the echo of steel wheels on rail, or the clang of ore carts in tunnels carved into the cliff faces.

When the boom ended, everything emptied out — but something stayed behind.

Sandon

Ironically called "the ghost town that refuses to die," Sandon still has scattered residents and restored buildings, but most of its bones are covered in moss and quiet. Visitors sometimes report:

- footsteps on the old boardwalks when no one is there

- lights in buildings that have no power

- the sudden smell of coal smoke

One photographer hiking through at dawn said the entire valley felt "expectant," like a theatre house before a performance.

Cody

Just east of Sandon, deeper in the valley, Cody is quieter — a handful of structures slumping into the forest.A hiker once reported seeing a figure in an old miner's coat stepping behind a collapsed building. When he walked over, the ground was undisturbed.

ANYOX — THE TOWN THAT VANISHED TWICE

A Company Town, a Dead Town, and Now a Haunted One

Anyox is one of BC's strangest forgotten places — a copper town on the north coast that was completely abandoned by 1935, then partially rebuilt, then abandoned *again*. Today it's only accessible by boat or charter, but explorers say the town feels preserved in a way that is unsettling.

Massive concrete structures — the powerhouse, smelter, and dam — loom like skeletal remains of an industrial empire swallowed by rainforest.

Visitors report:

- loud metal bangs echoing through the empty buildings

- footsteps on the catwalks above

- strange voices carried on the wind through the deep gorge

- lights reflecting off broken windows where no light source exists

One wilderness photographer described the atmosphere as:

"A feeling like someone is still up there working the night shift."

KITSUALT — THE GHOST TOWN THAT'S STILL PERFECT

Kitsault is different.Beautifully different.And eerily different.

Abandoned in 1982 after the molybdenum market collapsed, Kitsault isn't a ruin — it's pristine. Homes, sidewalks, streetlights, a hospital, a shopping mall, even playgrounds still stand intact. The lawns were mowed for years after abandonment.

People who've stayed overnight say the quiet is worse than in the ruined towns. There's no decay to soften the edges. Everything looks like it *should* be alive — but it isn't.

Several visitors report:

- hearing doors close in buildings where no wind enters

- lights flicking in buildings with no utilities connected

- the sense of being watched from upstairs windows

- the unmistakable feeling of a presence walking behind them down a hallway

Kitsault feels frozen — trapped between two eras — and that makes the silence heavy.

BLAKEBURN — WHERE THE MOUNTAIN TOOK THE TOWN

Near Princeton sits the long-dead mining community of Blakeburn, destroyed in 1930 when a massive explosion tore through the coal tunnels. Forty-five miners died underground. Locals say the explosion shook the entire valley.

To this day, hikers report:

- low rumbles from beneath the ground

- voices echoing faintly near collapsed shafts

- a feeling of being observed from the treeline

In one well-known incident, a pair of hikers claimed to hear the rhythmic clang of a pickaxe from deep underground — steady and slow — long after they realized the sound wasn't an echo from their own movements.

OCEAN FALLS — THE RAINIEST GHOST TOWN IN BC

Once home to 5,000 people and a massive pulp mill, Ocean Falls is now a strange mix of ruins, lone residents, and buildings surrendered to the rain — and the rain falls here harder than almost anywhere else in Canada.

Visitors often speak of:

- hearing voices in the empty apartment towers

- footsteps in the drowned streets

- strange shadows moving through the hallways of the old hospital

- a whistling sound no one can trace

The silence between the rainfall makes the place feel abandoned and alive at the same time.

THE SPIRIT OF THESE FORGOTTEN PLACES

What ties these ghost towns together isn't just abandonment. It's the sense that the land has absorbed everything — every argument in a saloon, every shift whistle, every death in a tunnel, every heartbeat from people who came west looking for a better life.

When you step into these valleys, the silence feels weighted.Not dangerous.Not threatening.Just *aware*.

You don't have to believe in ghosts to understand what these places feel like. Wilderness absorbs memory.Industrial ruins accelerate it.And BC has more of these forgotten towns than most countries do.

CASE FILES — MODERN REPORTS FROM BC GHOST TOWNS

Case File 17A — The Sandon Boardwalk Walker (2016)

A pair of hikers reported hearing distinct footsteps on the wooden walkway behind them. When they turned around, the footsteps stopped. No one else was in town at the time.

Case File 17B — The Kitsault Hospital Lights (2012)

Explorers witnessed lights flicking in several hospital rooms at dusk. Power has been disconnected for decades.

Case File 17C — The Blakeburn Echo (2004)

A backcountry camper reported repeated metallic strikes coming from underground at dawn. Geologists later confirmed no blasting or seismic activity.

Case File 17D — Anyox Catwalk Movement (2019)

A photographer reported hearing clear footsteps on a metal walkway above him in the old powerhouse. The building was locked behind him, and he was the only person there.

Ghost towns in British Columbia are not empty places.They're reminders — that the land keeps stories even when the people are gone.And that history, once rooted in the wilderness, doesn't simply fade away.

Some places remember.Some places echo.And some places whisper back when you listen too closely.

CHAPTER 18 — THE INDIGENOUS SPIRIT WORLD
Guardians, Warners & Shape-Shifters of British Columbia

If you spend enough time in the backcountry of British Columbia, it becomes impossible to ignore the feeling that the land is more than trees and rock and water. There are places where the atmosphere tightens without warning, as if the valley itself is watching. There are places where sound dies for no reason. There are moments when the forest seems to shift — not physically, but in a way you feel more than see.

For many modern hikers, those moments are unsettling.For Indigenous Nations across BC, those moments have names.

This chapter is not a collection of myths in the European fairy-tale sense. These are **spiritual beings**, **ancestral guardians**, **forest giants**, and **warners** that have shaped the relationships between humans and the wilderness here for thousands of years.

British Columbia has some of the richest spiritual landscapes in the world — and at its core is the understanding that the land is alive, aware, and responsive. That the wilderness is not empty, but inhabited by forces older than the first cedar that ever rooted in this soil.

These stories are not meant to frighten.They are meant to guide.

And in many cases, they overlap in extraordinary ways with the modern strange encounters that wilderness travelers still report today.

THE DZUNUKWA — THE WILD WOMAN OF THE WOODS

The Forest Giant Who Warns, Watches, and Sometimes Takes

Across many Coast Salish Nations, the *Dzunukwa* (sometimes spelled Dzoonokwa or Tsonoqua) is described as a towering forest being — not entirely human, not entirely animal — with deep black skin, wild hair, and eyes that glow like embers.

She is not the same as the Sasquatch, though outsiders often confuse them.She is older. More spiritual. Less physical.She exists in the boundary between the living world and the spirit one.

The *Dzunukwa* serves multiple roles:

- **a guardian of the deep forest**

- **a protector of sacred places**

- **a punisher of disrespectful travelers**

- **a bringer of wealth and power to those worthy**

- **and a stealer of children who wander too far**

Some stories portray her as monstrous, others as a misunderstood figure whose warnings are ignored by careless wanderers.

Many Elders describe her voice as hollow, almost wind-like — a sound travelers sometimes still report when hiking high ridges of Vancouver Island or the coastal ranges:a long, breathy call with no identifiable source.

THE SI'ATCO — THE FOREST GIANT THAT WALKS LIKE A MAN

Chehalis Teachings & the Origins of the Modern Sasquatch

The Chehalis people of the Fraser Valley carry the oldest known stories of the **Si'atco** — a large, hair-covered forest being that walks upright and avoids human contact.

Sound familiar? It should. This is the root of the English word **Sasquatch**, adapted from the Halq'eméylem term *sasq'ets*.

The Si'atco are not evil. They are not monsters. They are **keepers of the mountains** and **neighbors to humans**, though distant ones.

Chehalis Elders describe them as:

- shy

- powerful

- curious

- territorial when disrespected

- protectors of resource-rich valleys

- beings who avoid unnecessary harm

Many describe seeing them move silently through the trees — too fast for their size, too quiet for their weight.

One Elder I listened to years ago phrased it in a way that stuck with me:

"They are what happens when the forest decides to put legs under itself."

THE PUKWUDJIE & LITTLE PEOPLE OF THE INTERIOR

Tricksters, Mimics, and Harmless Watchers — Except When They Aren't

Among Interior Nations — including the Secwépemc, Nlaka'pamux, and some Carrier Sekani communities — there are stories of **small forest beings**, often benevolent but sometimes mischievous.

They appear as:

- tiny humanoids

- child-sized forest people

- shadows darting between stumps

- or voices imitating human children

Their purpose varies by region:

- they warn hunters of danger

- they mislead disrespectful travelers

- they protect certain mountains

- they mimic voices to lure people astray

Modern hikers in places like Wells Gray, the Nicola Valley, or the backcountry around Merritt sometimes report hearing:

- a child's voice

- a woman calling their name

- soft footsteps pacing the treeline

Search & Rescue teams often receive these reports during missing-person searches.

THE LAND OTTER PEOPLE — THE SEA SPIRITS OF THE NORTH COAST

Haida, Tsimshian & Nisga'a Lore Overlapping With Modern Coastal Sightings

On the northern coast — Prince Rupert, the Nass River, Haida Gwaii — the most powerful and feared supernatural beings are the **Land Otter People**, known by various names across Nations.

They are shapeshifters tied to death, water, and the boundary between worlds.They appear as:

- humans with otter-like faces

- people without footprints

- figures standing on the tide line at dusk

- drowned souls transformed by the sea

In many stories, they lure people using familiar voices.They are not malicious, but they are **not human**, and mistakes happen.

What makes these stories remarkable is that modern coastal residents — fishermen, loggers, boaters, beach campers — still report encounters with:

- human-shaped figures on remote beaches

- footprints that start or end at the waterline

- drowning victims seen standing upright in surf

- voices calling from fogbanks

Even if one doesn't take the stories literally, they reveal a deep understanding of how dangerous and deceptive the Pacific coast can be.

THE BUKWUS — THE FOREST SPIRIT OF LONELINESS

The "Wild Man of the Woods" Who Appears to Those at the Edge

Bukwus is a ghost-like forest spirit in Kwakwaka'wakw tradition — thin, wandering, hungry, living between the worlds of the living and the dead.

He appears to:

- lost travelers

- emotionally broken people

- those suffering from grief

- people in danger of becoming "lost souls" themselves

His presence is not malevolent, but heavy.He offers food — rotten food — as a test.To accept it is to join him.

What's fascinating is how many modern hikers describe moments of sudden despair, fear, or hopelessness in specific valleys or ridges, as if the landscape itself is pushing them to emotional breaking. Many Indigenous Elders say these are **Bukwus valleys** — places where sorrow clings.

THE MIMICS — VOICES THAT SHOULD NOT EXIST

The Most Universally Reported Mystery Across BC Nations

Nearly every Nation in BC shares some version of a being that **mimics voices**:

- a loved one

- a child

- a hunting partner

- someone calling for help

These beings lure people off trails or deeper into dangerous valleys.In most stories, the mimic never attacks — it simply leads the person far from safety.

This aligns startlingly with modern vanishings:

- people stepping off a trail as if following someone

- hikers insisting they heard a partner call to them

- search subjects walking toward phantom voices

SAR members sometimes acknowledge this phenomenon informally: *"sound that shouldn't be coming from where it's coming from."*

Indigenous stories simply named it thousands of years earlier.

THE OVERLAP WITH MODERN WILDERNESS MYSTERIES

Where Ancient Stories and Modern Encounters Intersect

For someone like me — someone who investigates sightings, interviews witnesses, and spends far too many nights in the bush — the most striking thing about Indigenous teachings is how much they resonate with real modern reports.

Consider the overlaps:

- glowing eyes in deep forest → **Dzunukwa / Forest Giants**

- tall upright figures at dusk → **Si'atco / Sasquatch**

- voices calling your name → **Mimics**

- sudden despair or emotional collapse → **Bukwus**

- figures on beaches during fog → **Land Otter People**

- small shadows moving through underbrush → **Little People**

You don't need to interpret them literally to feel their value. These stories were built from thousands of years of lived experience, observation, and survival in this landscape.

They are not warnings to avoid the wilderness. They are warnings to **respect** it.

CASE FILES — MODERN REPORTS WITH SPIRIT-WORLD PARALLELS

Case File 18A — The Vancouver Island Voice (2014)

Two campers near Port Renfrew heard a woman calling for help. They followed the voice for nearly fifteen minutes before realizing it never got closer or farther — it drifted *laterally*, always just beyond the next cedar. No missing-person cases were active at the time.

Case File 18B — The Nass River Beach Figure (2011)

A fisherman saw a person standing ankle-deep in surf at dusk. When he shouted, the figure walked straight into the waves and vanished.

Case File 18C — The Interior Child's Laugh (2020)

A hunter in the Nicola Valley heard a child giggling behind a stump. The nearest homes were 20 km away. Tracks showed no small prints.

Case File 18D — The Lone Giant of Chehalis (2007)

A forester saw a tall figure near a clear-cut boundary watching him. When he signalled, the figure took two steps and disappeared behind a massive cedar that could not physically conceal something that size.

BC's spirit world is not about ghosts haunting abandoned places.It's about a **living, breathing wilderness** with its own rules, its own guardians, and its own boundaries.

And if there's one thing every Elder — from Vancouver Island to the Nass, from Chilcotin to the Columbia — agrees on, it's this:

"You don't walk these lands alone without being seen.The forest knows you're there long before you know it's watching."

CHAPTER 19 — HAUNTED WATERS OF BRITISH COLUMBIA
Ghosts, Lost Ships, Drowned Voices & Lakes That Never Give Back

Water behaves differently in British Columbia.It carries memory.It holds stories.And in some places, it refuses to let go of the dead.

I've always believed that a forest can feel alive, but in BC, the lakes and coastlines often feel *aware*. There are stretches of ocean where fishermen refuse to drop anchor, rivers that choke with silence at dusk, and lakes so deep and black that locals warn newcomers not to whistle near them after dark.

When you speak to long-time residents — loggers, boat captains, lighthouse keepers, and Indigenous Elders — one message repeats:

"These waters have their own moods. Their own rules."

And sometimes, their own ghosts.

This chapter explores the stranger side of BC's lakes, rivers, and coastline — the sightings, legends, drownings, phantom vessels, and water spirits that continue to bleed across modern reports.

Not as folklore.Not as campfire stories.But as lived experiences, documented across generations.

THE LADY OF OKANAGAN LAKE

A Woman in White Who Walks the Shoreline Before Tragedy

Ogopogo may be Okanagan Lake's most famous resident, but it isn't the only one.

For over a century, people have reported seeing a woman in a pale dress walking the lakeshore — sometimes barefoot, sometimes gliding just above the ground — almost always near spots where drownings occur.

Witnesses claim her features are indistinct.They say she doesn't react when approached.She simply walks the shoreline until she fades.

In one chilling account from 1984, a group camping near Peachland woke to the sound of a woman crying softly along the rocks. When they shone their flashlights, the figure dissolved into the mist. The next morning, RCMP were searching for a missing teenager whose canoe had overturned hours earlier.

Locals say she is a **harbinger**, not a ghost — a warning presence tied to the lake's darker moods.

THE HAUNTED WATERS OF SHUSWAP LAKE

Phantom Campfires, Distant Drums & Ghost Canoes

Shuswap is a place of deep ridges, hidden bays, and sudden fog banks that sweep in silently. It also holds some of the oldest water spirit traditions in BC.

Multiple houseboat operators have reported strange nighttime encounters:

- **campfires on islands that vanish when approached**

- **drumming from somewhere across the water at 2 a.m.**

- **canoes drifting with no paddlers, then dissolving into mist**

- **shadows moving along cliffs where no trails exist**

One veteran boater recalled seeing a fire on Copper Island in 2011. Four figures sat around it, unmoving. When he idled closer, the fire winked out — and the shoreline was completely dark.

During low tourist seasons, the lake takes on an eerie stillness, as though an older world rises just beneath the surface.

LAKE COWICHAN'S DROWNED VOICES

A Vancouver Island Mystery That Never Truly Fades

Lake Cowichan is known for its beauty, but it also has a long history of drownings — far more than you'd expect for a recreational lake.

Local residents have long claimed the water "speaks" at night.Campers report:

- distant voices calling from the center of the lake

- soft splashes with no visible cause

- conversations in indistinguishable languages drifting over calm water

- children laughing after midnight when no boats are out

Several Indigenous Elders say the lake is inhabited by **water spirits who mimic voices**, drawing people toward the shoreline.

One fisherman told me in 2015:

"You'll hear someone say your name across the water.You look around, and there's no one.The lake is teasing you — calling you closer."

He paused."And that's how people disappear."

THE QUEEN CHARLOTTE SOUND GHOST SHIP

A Vessel of Light Seen Where No Ship Should Be

North of Vancouver Island, the waters become wilder, colder, and less forgiving. In this region, mariners have reported sightings of a **phantom ship** for decades — a glowing vessel drifting silently against the wind.

Fishermen describe it as:

- tall-masted

- bright white

- no sound

- no wake

- disappearing when approached

Canadian Coast Guard logs contain several informal notes referring to "unexplained lights offshore," though no official file acknowledges the phenomenon.

In 2006, three crab fishermen near Calvert Island saw what they thought was a schooner in distress — lights flickering through sea fog. When they raced toward it, the ship faded slowly into darkness, leaving nothing but rolling water.

Elders from the Heiltsuk Nation say the ghost ship is a **warning**, a reminder of the hundreds lost in the region's brutal storms long before the first lighthouse was ever built.

THE HAUNTED LIGHTHOUSE AT RACE ROCKS

The Keeper Who Never Left His Post

Off southern Vancouver Island near Victoria sits Race Rocks — a brutal, wind-lashed passage where the ocean funnels unpredictably. The lighthouse there has one of the oldest ghost stories in BC.

A former keeper drowned in the 1920s after being swept from the rocks during a storm. Since then, numerous keepers, students, and marine station workers have reported:

- heavy bootsteps in the tower

- a figure seen pacing the balcony during fog

- the lighthouse door opening by itself

- lights turning on despite no power

- a man's voice murmuring on the stairwell

One marine biology student wrote in her field log in 1999:

"Someone walked past me on the lower level.I turned to say hello — but the room was empty."

Veteran keepers simply say:"Some lighthouses never lose their keepers."

THE RESTLESS DEPTHS OF WILLISTON LAKE

A Flooded Valley & A Spirit-Drenched Reservoir

When the W.A.C. Bennett Dam created Williston Lake — one of the largest reservoirs in North America — hundreds of valleys, villages, burial grounds, and forests were drowned under its surface.

Since then, boaters and locals have described:

- **trees rising from below like hands**

- **voices echoing across the water at dusk**

- **strange lights deep under the surface**

- **shadowy forms pacing on old submerged roads**

Some Elders believe the reservoir disrupted ancient resting places.Others say the spirits were always there, and we simply flooded their home.

A guide in Hudson's Hope described the lake this way:

"That water holds an entire world beneath it.You can feel it when you're out in the middle —like you're floating above someone else's memories."

THE HAUNTED SHORES OF HAIDA GWAII

Where the Boundary Between Living & Spirit Is Thin

Haida Gwaii has always been a place of immense spiritual energy — a land where ocean, forest, and supernatural beings coexist. The waters here, especially near abandoned villages and longhouses, teem with stories.

Visitors report:

- **voices drifting from empty beaches**

- **canoe-like shapes gliding along moonlit surf**

- **women singing in Haida language near ancient totem sites**

- **blue-white lights skipping across tide pools**

One kayaker camping near Tanu Island described waking at dawn to the sound of drumbeats far across the water. When he paddled out, the noise ceased instantly. He turned toward shore — and saw a dark shape watching from the treeline.

He didn't camp alone again.

CASE FILES — MODERN HAUNTINGS OF BC'S WATERS

Case File 19A — The Shuswap Phantom Fire (2018)

Houseboaters saw a bright campfire on Copper Island around midnight.When they landed, the fire vanished — leaving cold, untouched ground.

Case File 19B — The Okanagan Shoreline Walker (1994)

A couple saw a pale woman drifting along the rocks near Peachland.She vanished behind a boulder.A drowning recovery began the next morning.

Case File 19C — The Williston Voices (2007)

Two anglers heard muffled conversation coming from beneath their boat.The water was over 90 metres deep.

Case File 19D — The Land Otter Beach Figure (2020)

A fisherman on Graham Island saw a person standing ankle-deep in fog.When he approached, the figure folded into the mist like smoke.

WHY BC'S WATERS FEEL HAUNTED

Because they are.Not in the Hollywood sense — but in the sense that water is memory.It keeps what it takes.It gives back only when it chooses.And in British Columbia, the waterways run deeper than the physical world.

Here, lakes have moods.Rivers hold stories.And the coastline has a voice — one that never entirely fades.

If forests are where BC watches you,then the water is where BC remembers you.

CHAPTER 20 — FRONTIER LEGENDS & STRANGE HISTORICAL EVENTS

Ghost Trails, Phantom Travelers & the Unfinished Stories of Early British Columbia

British Columbia's frontier history reads like a collision between two worlds — the Indigenous world that had been here for thousands of years, and the sudden arrival of miners, telegraph workers, prospectors, pack-train drivers, and surveyors. These early outsiders stepped into a landscape that was older, deeper, and far less forgiving than they realized.

Much of the province's settlement history is recorded in newspapers and archives. But the *other* history — the one whispered in bunkhouses, passed between trappers, or scribbled in half-legible survey journals — is just as important.

These strange stories didn't make the official books.They weren't meant to.

These are the tales of travelers who saw figures walking beside rivers that no one else could see… of old telegraph lines that hummed long after power was gone… of prospectors who vanished between two points only a mile apart… and of entire pack trains that reportedly heard footsteps pacing behind them for days.

This chapter is about what happens when determined people push into land they don't fully understand — and what the wilderness gives back in return.

THE TELEGRAPH TRAIL GHOSTS

Voices on the Line & Travelers Who Never Arrived

Before BC had highways, it had telegraph lines — fragile strands of wire stretched across impossible wilderness, from the coast through the mountains and up into the Interior. The men who maintained these lines often worked alone for weeks, carrying food on their backs, sleeping in rough shacks, and following the thin trail carved beneath the wires.

Years later, long after the lines went silent, hikers have reported strange experiences on these same trails:

- hearing faint Morse-like tapping from nowhere

- seeing a man walking the trail ahead, only for him to disappear behind a cedar

- the sensation of someone matching their pace just beyond the treeline

Some of these accounts match older stories from the 1880s and 1890s, when telegraph workers themselves wrote of odd encounters:

The 1897 Hazelton Journal

A lineman described waking at night to the sound of someone walking around his cabin. When he opened the door, no footprints marked the fresh snow. He wrote:

"I was not alone that night, yet no man or animal had come.I heard what I heard."

The Cassiar Echo Case

Another worker near the Cassiar line wrote of hearing the telegraph wires vibrating violently — even though the line had been severed days earlier in a storm.

THE PHANTOM PACK TRAINS OF THE CARIBOO

Horses That Saw What Their Riders Couldn't

The Cariboo Gold Rush brought thousands into BC's Interior, most of them traveling by long pack trains along narrow, exposed trails. The animals — especially horses and mules — often sensed danger long before the men.

There are dozens of accounts of horses:

- stopping dead on a trail

- refusing to cross certain creeks

- backing away from empty, silent stretches of timber

- shying violently at unseen obstacles

Many old-timers swore that animals reacted to "ghost travelers" — the spirits of prospectors who died alone on the trail and were never recovered.

One of the most famous tales came from a packer near Barkerville who claimed a mule named Jasper refused to walk past a specific ravine. The animal trembled and backed up, even when coaxed. When the packer stepped ahead alone, he felt a sudden wave of dread and the sensation of someone standing directly behind him.

He turned around.No one.But Jasper was staring past him, ears locked forward, eyes wide.

The packer later learned that several years earlier, a prospector had vanished in that exact spot. His body was never found.

THE SALMON ARM CAMPFIRE VISITOR

A Frontier Story Too Strange to Ignore

In the early 1900s, two surveyors working near Salmon Arm camped beside the lake. They were eating supper when a man stepped into their firelight — soaked, silent, staring.

He wore clothing decades out of date.He did not speak.He simply looked at them, then at the fire, then toward the water.When one of the surveyors rose to offer help, the man stepped backward... and faded into the darkness.

The next morning, they found footprints leading toward the lake, then ending abruptly on wet stones.

Old loggers later told them the story of a lost steamboat passenger who drowned in the lake years earlier — last seen struggling near that same shoreline.

THE VANISHED PROSPECTORS OF THE STEWART REGION

Stories That Refused to Be Buried

Northern BC was full of prospectors seeking fortunes in valleys no one had mapped. Some succeeded. Many disappeared. A few left behind mysteries that locals still talk about.

The Man Who Walked Into the Glacier (1913)

Near Stewart, a prospector was last seen entering a small ice tunnel at the foot of a glacier. When he didn't return, others followed his tracks — they led into the tunnel, then stopped in a chamber with no other exit.

The air was still.The snow unmoved.His lantern was found extinguished on the ground.His body was never found.

The Two Prospector Camps (1921)

Two men working near the Portland Canal vanished from their camp.A search party found:

- their tools neatly stacked

- food cooking on a stove

- bedrolls still warm

- no footprints leaving the site

Snowfall had begun minutes earlier, suggesting the men had disappeared seconds before the search team arrived.

THE HAUNTED TRAILS OF KASLO & THE VALHALLAS

Shadow Figures, Whistling Winds & Travelers Who Felt Followed

The Valhalla Range is among BC's most rugged wilderness areas — steep granite walls, deep basins, waterfalls like white scars running down cliffs.

Hikers here often describe:

- a sudden sense of being watched

- hearing footsteps behind them on talus paths

- a dark figure slipping between old cedars

- a strange whistling wind that sounds like someone inhaling

One old trail story involves a logger who walked the same route every day.For weeks, he heard someone whistling behind him — never close, never far. When he turned, the sound would stop instantly. One morning, he stopped in a clearing and said aloud:

"If you're following me, follow me in daylight."

That day, the whistling returned — but now in front of him.

He never took that trail again.

THE "MISSING BETWEEN TWO POINTS" CASES

Frontier Disappearances That Never Made Sense

Even in the 1800s, people were vanishing in ways that didn't add up. The most troubling cases involved individuals who disappeared between two known points within short distances:

- a trapper walked from a cabin to a creek and never arrived

- a miner walked between two tunnels less than 300 metres apart and vanished

- a ranch hand disappeared crossing an open field in view of others

- a telegraph worker vanished between line stations during clear weather

In one case from 1904, a prospector walking behind his partner disappeared around a slight bend in the trail. When the partner reached the bend, the trail ahead was empty — fresh snow showed only one set of footprints.

His.Not the man who vanished.

THE BOUNDARY BETWEEN HISTORY & THE UNEXPLAINED

The striking thing about these frontier stories is how much they resemble modern wilderness mysteries:

- footsteps with no visible source

- disappearances in impossible circumstances

- animals reacting to unseen presences

- voices calling from ahead on the trail

- strange sounds that mimic human language

- figures glimpsed at the edge of firelight

BC's frontier wasn't just a rugged wilderness — it was a place where people were constantly stepping into lands rich with spiritual, geological, and psychological power.

The stories they left behind aren't just folklore.They're warnings.Echoes of lessons learned too late.

Because the wilderness of British Columbia isn't just vast — it's ancient.And some stories refuse to stay buried.

CHAPTER 21 — THE SUPERNATURAL COASTLINE
Where Fog Walks, Spirits Drift, and the Ocean Remembers Everything

There is something fundamentally different about the coastline of British Columbia. The interior has its forests, mountains, giants, mimics, and disappearances — but the coast has an older kind of strangeness. A *tidal* strangeness. A weirdness shaped by salt, storms, and the vast pull of the Pacific.

Anyone who has spent real time here — Haida Gwaii, Prince Rupert, the Nass River, the Broughton Archipelago, Bella Bella, the inlets of the Central Coast — knows this:

The coastline feels alive. Not metaphorically.Not romantically.Literally alive.

It watches.It whispers.It shifts in ways that make you question your senses.

The ocean creates its own kind of silence — a silence layered over rolling surf, foghorn moans, gull cries, and the distant thump of waves against rock. And beneath that soundscape is a presence, something older than memory, older than the first cedar tree that ever rooted in BC's soil.

This chapter explores that strange presence — the ghosts, spirits, phantom lights, and unexplainable encounters that haunt one of the most spiritually charged coastlines on Earth.

THE NAAS RIVER — BC'S MOST HAUNTED WATERWAY

Where the Dead Walk in Fog and Spirits Claim Their Tides

The Nass River valley is a place where the line between the living and the spirit world is *thin*.Very thin.

Nisga'a Elders have always said the fog here is not just weather — it is **a carrier of spirits**, a medium the dead move through. Hunters, fishermen, and travelers speak with a kind of quiet respect when describing this valley.

Modern reports include:

- **humanoid shapes walking on tidal flats at low tide, then vanishing when approached**

- **voices drifting across the river at night despite no nearby camps**

- **eyes reflecting back from fog banks far from shore**

- **figures seen standing on gravel bars that disappear seconds later**

One fisherman told me that the Nass feels "crowded" even when he's alone. Not threatening — just **inhabited**.

HAIDA GWAII — THE EDGE OF THE WORLD & THE THIN PLACE BETWEEN WORLDS

The Land Where Every Island Has a Ghost Story

Haida Gwaii is steeped in supernatural energy.Not spooky.Not haunted in the Hollywood sense.More like *charged* — a place where everything hums a little differently.

Here, you find:

- shadow figures pacing beaches at dusk

- glowing orbs drifting between ancient fallen longhouses

- disembodied singing in Haida language coming from empty shoreline villages

- phantom canoes gliding across moonlit surf

- lights skipping over tide pools like fireflies in slow motion

One kayaker camping near Tanu heard what sounded like a paddling rhythm, slow and steady, just beyond the fog. When he shone his light, he saw nothing — but the rhythmic splashing continued, moving parallel to shore.

He didn't sleep that night.

Elders say the spirits of abandoned Haida villages still walk at dawn. Not malicious — simply returning to the places they once lived.

THE SKEENA COAST — LIGHTS, SHADOWS, AND THE NOISES THAT SHOULDN'T EXIST

A Coastline That Shifts Beneath You

Between Prince Rupert, Port Edward, and the mouth of the Skeena, the coast is a labyrinth of islands, channels, logging roads, and industrial ruins.

This is where some of the strangest modern reports originate:

Phantom Lights

Bright, white-blue lights that:

- drift just above treeline

- hover over water

- appear in clusters on uninhabited islands

- vanish the moment a boat approaches

These aren't boat lights.Aren't aircraft.Aren't flares.The Coast Guard has logged dozens of such "unconfirmed visual anomalies."

Shadow Walkers

Longshore workers report seeing tall shapes moving through fog banks, pacing in and out of view. One tugboat captain said he watched a figure standing on the rocks — a silhouette with no headlamp, no gear, no movement — in a place a person physically couldn't stand.

When he blinked, the figure was gone.

BELLA BELLA & THE BUBBLE CLOUD SPIRITS

A Central Coast Mystery That Defies Explanation

Near Bella Bella, several generations of Heiltsuk residents have reported what they call "bubble clouds" — glowing, spherical masses of light that float beneath the water like submerged lanterns.

These lights:

- drift against current

- move slowly in pairs

- rise toward boats

- vanish instantly when touched by oar or paddle

Kayakers describe seeing something watching them from beneath the surface — not an animal, but a round, pulsing glow.

One Elder told me:

"These are not creatures. These are watchers. They see who passes."

VANCOUVER ISLAND'S WEST COAST — THE SHADOW COASTLINE

Shipwreck Spirits, Lighthouse Ghosts & the Strange Silence After Midnight

The stretch from Bamfield to Tofino is known as the **Graveyard of the Pacific** — hundreds of shipwrecks, storms that rise out of nowhere, and more ghost-lore than anywhere else in BC.

The Ghost of Pachena Bay

Campers report:

- a woman calling for help from the surf

- footsteps running behind tents

- heavy thumps on the beach like someone falling from a height

Nuu-chah-nulth stories describe a spirit who warns travelers of tidal danger. Locals believe this presence still walks the shore.

The Lighthouse Keepers Who Never Left

From Carmanah to Pachena to Amphitrite Point, keepers have reported:

- knocking on locked doors

- voices on empty stairwells

- the sound of boots climbing metal ladders

- figures seen staring from dark windows of unoccupied keepers' quarters

And it isn't just history — recent volunteers have filed identical experiences.

THE SUNSHINE COAST & THE WHISPERING INLETS

Marine Spirits That Move on Still Water

The Sunshine Coast seems peaceful, but deep in the inlets of Sechelt, Narrows Inlet, and Tzoonie, the atmosphere changes.

Visitors report:

- whispers echoing across perfectly calm water

- the sound of paddles striking water nearby — with no canoe in sight

- long, human-like shadows sliding beneath clear tidal shallows

Indigenous teachings say that certain inlets contain **invisible travelers** — spirits who move through coastal pathways long before boats existed.

TEXADA ISLAND — THE COAST'S MOST UNDERRATED HAUNTING

Saltwater Ghost Towns, Mine Spirits & Coastal Shadows

Texada Island has a surprisingly dark supernatural history:

- phantom miners seen walking into sealed shafts

- lights drifting above the ocean cliffs

- footsteps following hikers along old wagon routes

- strange metallic knocking beneath the ground

One miner's cabin near Gillies Bay has produced dozens of reports of a figure standing at the foot of the bed — tall, silent, unmoving — fading the moment the witness sits up.

The island is full of abandoned industrial sites, and even casual visitors say Texada has "an energy" that's impossible to shake.

CASE FILES — REPORTS FROM BC'S SUPERNATURAL COASTLINE

Case File 21A — The Nass Fog Walker (2015)

A man fishing alone saw a tall figure walking through fog on a gravel bar.When he shouted, the figure dissolved into the mist.

Case File 21B — The Haida Singing (2002)

A pair of kayakers camped on Lyell Island heard women singing far offshore.There were no boats.The sound lasted for nearly an hour.

Case File 21C — The Bella Bella Lights (2018)

A group of youth witnessed two bright spheres drifting beneath their canoe, illuminating the water.They vanished instantly when touched.

Case File 21D — The Skeena Cliff Figure (2010)

A tugboat captain saw a human silhouette standing on an impossible cliff ledge.When he blinked, it was gone.

WHY THE COAST FEELS DIFFERENT

Because it *is* different.There are few places on Earth where ancient Indigenous supernatural traditions overlap so seamlessly with modern reports.

On BC's coast:

- water is memory

- fog is a boundary

- islands hold stories

- lights behave unpredictably

- the forest meets the sea with no warning

- spirits move through tides, storms, and shorelines

The land doesn't just watch you.The ocean does too.

And sometimes, late at night, when the tide is low and the fog begins to rise, you feel the truth older than any map:

On the coast of British Columbia, you are never truly alone.

CHAPTER 22 — WOODS THAT WATCH
Forest Spirits, Living Trees & the Places That Don't Want You There

There are forests in British Columbia that feel different the moment you step into them.Some places simply *are* forest — soil, roots, cedar, fir, rain, wind.But others… others feel like stepping into someone's home uninvited.

You feel watched.Not threatened — not immediately — but *noticed*.As if the forest hasn't decided yet whether to tolerate you or turn against you.

Every wilderness researcher eventually learns to tell the difference.

I've walked enough BC timber to know that the land has moods. Some places feel open and warm. But then there are valleys where the air grows tight, where sound dies without reason, where shadows lean the wrong way, and where you instinctively check behind you even when you know you're alone.

This chapter dives into those places — the ones locals warn each other about, the ones Elders speak of carefully, and the ones hikers only visit once.

These aren't ghost towns.They aren't creature sightings.They are *living forests* — places that watch, remember, and react.

THE SILENT FORESTS

Where Sound Goes to Die

Silence in the wilderness is normal — wind drops, birds calm, predators pass, weather changes.But the **wrong kind of silence** is unmistakable.

It comes suddenly.Completely.Like a blanket dropped over the world.

Veteran hikers across BC report sudden dead zones in places like:

- Lynn Headwaters back basins

- deep Garibaldi side valleys

- the Telkwa high forests

- sections of the Skagit

- the Ashlu side drainages

- old-growth pockets near Knight Inlet

- Vancouver Island's interior cedar swamps

In these zones:

- birds stop

- insects stop

- wind seems to stop

- even your own footsteps feel muffled

Search & Rescue teams have their own term for it:**"unnatural quiet."**

Indigenous Elders have a different description:**"The land is listening to you."**

THE SHADOWS THAT MOVE WRONG

Not Faster. Not Slower. Wrong.

In certain BC forests, shadows behave strangely.This is one of the most consistent reports from hunters, Elders, and solo hikers.

People describe:

- shadows that move against the light

- figures sliding between trees that vanish instantly

- a human-shaped darkness leaning behind a stump

- silhouettes pacing treelines at dusk

- dark shapes drifting *above* the forest floor

These aren't full apparitions. They're more like impressions — as if something passed through the corner of your vision and refused to be fully seen.

One backcountry ranger near Bella Coola reported:

"The shadows felt heavy, like they had weight.I kept waiting for something to step out.It never did.But it watched."

He refused to camp in that valley again.

THE DO-NOT-ENTER GROVES

Elders Know These Forests. And They Avoid Them.

Across BC, Indigenous communities identify certain pockets of forest as dangerous or spiritually charged. These aren't myths — these are long-standing survival teachings based on thousands of years of lived experience.

These groves usually share traits:

- unusually tight tree spacing

- thick moss that swallows sound

- twisted cedar formations

- sudden cold spots

- an immediate instinct to turn back

Some areas are known as:

- **"places of watchers"**

- **"the listening woods"**

- **"the forest where you do not speak"**

- **"the mourning valleys"**

One Elder from the Interior said:

"You do not go in there unless you want the forest to follow you home."

When asked what she meant, she simply replied:"Some places don't forget you."

THE FEELING OF BEING FOLLOWED

The Most Common Modern Report — Across the Entire Province

If there's one experience nearly every solo hiker has in BC eventually, it's this:

You're walking a remote trail.The air changes.You feel someone behind you.You stop.The feeling stops.You walk again.Something matches your pace, just out of sight.

This phenomenon is reported in:

- the Stein Valley

- northern Vancouver Island

- Manning Park

- Haida Gwaii

- the Kootenays

- upper Squamish valleys

- the old Stikine trails

- anywhere near abandoned logging grades

What makes it unsettling is not sound — often, nothing makes noise.It's presence.A weight.An awareness.

Hunters say it feels like a large animal shadowing them, but without footfalls.Elders say it's the spirit of the valley acknowledging your presence.SAR says it's "hyper-vigilance triggered by terrain."But many people insist it's something else entirely.

One hiker near Gold River described it perfectly:

"Something was matching my steps.Not copying them — *following* them."

THE MIMICKING FORESTS

Voices Where No Voices Exist

We talked about mimics in Indigenous lore — beings that can imitate human voices.But modern hikers still report:

- hearing their own names whispered

- hearing a partner calling from ahead when that partner is behind

- hearing a child crying deep in timber

- hearing footsteps out of sync with their own

- hearing someone say "hey" from ten feet into a bushwall

Almost always, these voices come from:

- dense cedar groves

- long, narrow valleys

- fog-heavy forests

- areas near old growth

- moss flats

SAR teams receive these reports quietly, often from missing-persons who were later recovered alive but shaken.

One survivor near Pitt Lake said:

"Someone kept saying 'this way' in a soft voice.I followed it.If I hadn't stopped, I would've walked off a cliff."

Whether psychological or paranormal, the effect is the same:The forest leads — and people follow.

THE TREE-LINE WATCHERS

Figures Seen on Ridges at Dusk

Across BC, dozens of reports describe human-shaped figures standing still at the tree-line — observing hikers from afar.

They are always:

- tall

- motionless

- dark

- silent

- seen just once

And always gone by the time anyone looks again.

These figures don't move.They don't approach.They simply watch.

A climber near Joffre Lakes described seeing a tall silhouette standing on a snow ridge against fading light:

"It looked like a person. Not a bear.When I blinked, it was gone.No tracks."

THE FORESTS THAT FEEL OLDER THAN TIME

Places Where You Walk Softly Without Knowing Why

Some parts of BC feel ancient in a way you can't articulate.Places where the air seems thicker, where every step feels like it presses into history.

Examples include:

- the old-growth of Meares Island

- the Cathedral Grove giants

- the Haida Gwaii cedar forests

- the deep Fraser canyon groves

- the Incomappleux Valley remnant rainforest

- untouched valleys of the Great Bear Rainforest

Walk here long enough and you feel it — not fear, but reverence.

A sense that something preceded youand will outlast youand is considering whether you're worth acknowledging.

CASE FILES — THE FORESTS THAT WATCH BACK

Case File 22A — The Gold River Step-Matcher (2013)

A hiker repeatedly felt someone walking behind him.He stopped sixteen times.Each time, the feeling stopped instantly.He completed the hike but refused to return alone.

Case File 22B — The Knight Inlet Shadow (2019)

A solo kayaker camping inland saw a tall shadow standing between two cedars at dusk.He approached.The shadow slid sideways — then vanished.

Case File 22C — The Ashlu Whispering Trees (2017)

A pair of trail runners heard a soft "hey" from ten feet off-trail.No one was there.No animal tracks.No wind.

Case File 22D — The Lynn Headwaters Silence Pocket (2010)

SAR reported losing all radio transmission in a 30-metre section of forest.Birdsong returned only when they stepped out of the zone.

WHY THESE WOODS WATCH

The answer depends on who you ask.

Elders say the forests watch because they are alive — spiritually, metaphorically, and in ways science doesn't yet understand.

Hunters say it's predator instinct — something large, quiet, and curious.

SAR teams say it's terrain psychology.

Hikers say it's presence — that feeling of being observed in a place not meant for you.

I say it's all of it.And something else, too.

Because in British Columbia, the forest doesn't just surround you.It recognizes you.It appraises you.And it decides how it feels about you.

When BC's woods watch, they aren't judging.They're simply remembering.

And you never truly walk away unseen.

CHAPTER 23 — CASE FILES OF THE UNEXPLAINED
BC's Strangest Modern Reports

British Columbia has no shortage of wilderness mysteries — Sasquatch encounters, haunted waters, vanished hikers, forest spirits, mimicking voices. But some cases stand apart from the rest. They don't fit into any category. They don't match Indigenous spirit lore, creature sightings, or Search & Rescue patterns. They simply sit in that uncomfortable space where the rational mind runs out of track.

These are the reports people hesitate to share.The ones they keep to themselves for months — sometimes years — afraid of being dismissed or laughed at. But when they finally speak, the details are strangely consistent with hundreds of others across the province.

This chapter isn't about proving the supernatural.It's about presenting the encounters that defy neat explanations — the ones that feel like the forest, the land, or the coastline briefly showed its deeper layers.

Each of these cases comes from regular people: loggers, hikers, teachers, students, hunters, fishermen, backroad travelers, and families on camping trips. None of them wanted attention. None were looking for the strange. They simply ran into it.

CASE FILE CATEGORY I — THE WATCHERS

Sightings of Figures That Shouldn't Exist

Across BC, people still report seeing tall, dark figures standing motionless at the edge of tree lines. Not Sasquatch-sized. Not animal-shaped. Just... human-shaped shadows that stand too still, too silently, and vanish the instant you look away.

Case File 23A — The Elaho Valley Looker (2018)

A pair of climbers descending a ridge saw a dark figure watching from a slope about 200 metres away. It stood with perfect stillness — no sway, no shifting. When they raised binoculars, the figure was gone. Snow showed no tracks.

Case File 23B — The Kootenay Switchback Sentinel (2021)

A logging truck driver, rounding a high switchback at dawn, saw what he thought was a person standing on a cliff edge in work clothes. The "person" turned slightly — then dissolved like smoke. The driver braked so hard he left skid marks.

Case File 23C — Vancouver Island Timberline Figure (2016)

A hunter glassing a distant ridge near Gold River saw a silhouette leaning against a cedar trunk. When he hiked to the spot, the ground was untouched.

These figures are always described the same way:

- tall

- dark

- silent

- watching

- gone instantly

No tracks.No smell.No sound.Just a presence — a momentary reminder that we are not alone in BC's wild places.

CASE FILE CATEGORY II — THE PHANTOM SOUNDS

Noise Without Source: Voices, Footsteps, and Drums

BC's wilderness has no shortage of natural noises — wind through fir needles, ravens calling, water hitting rocks. But these sounds are different. They imitate human patterns with eerie accuracy.

Case File 23D — The Bella Coola Steps (2014)

A photographer heard someone walking behind him on soft moss for nearly an hour. Every time he stopped, the footsteps stopped. Every time he moved, they resumed — perfectly matched. No one was found on the trail.

Case File 23E — Garibaldi Valley Drums (2019)

A pair of experienced hikers reported hearing distant drumming echoing across an alpine basin. There were no trails, no camps, and no bodies of water to carry sound that far.

Case File 23F — The Terrace Forest Voice (2020)

A mushroom picker heard a woman calling "Hello?" repeatedly from different angles, as if circling him. He packed up and left immediately.

Often these reports mention:

- no echo

- no directionality

- no response when called back

- an uncanny "hollowness" to the sound

CASE FILE CATEGORY III — MISSING TIME

The Strangest Reports of All

A dozen BC residents over the years have described missing time in the backcountry — not hours, but minutes. Sometimes just enough to disorient them.

Case File 23G — The Chilliwack River Gap (2015)

A hiker checked his GPS at a trail junction. Five minutes later, he checked again — and nearly an hour had passed. His track log showed he had walked 1.8 km during that missing hour, but he had no memory of doing it.

Case File 23H — The Squamish Lost Moment (2022)

A climber rappelling off a ridge looked down, blinked — and was suddenly at the base of the cliff, rope coiled neatly beside him. He didn't remember the descent.

Case File 23I — Nass Valley Drift (2017)

A hunter sitting on a rock to rest blinked and found himself standing ten feet away in thick brush. He didn't recall moving.

These reports are rare — but unnerving.

CASE FILE CATEGORY IV — THE FOREST LIGHTS

Drifting Globes, Vertical Beams & Lights That Move Like Intelligence

The "orb" phenomenon is global, but BC seems to have its own unique version — lights that move with purpose.

Case File 23J — Haida Gwaii Blue Globes (2021)

Campers saw two blue-white lights drifting between trees near their camp. They hovered at chest height, circled each other, then vanished like sparks blown out.

Case File 23K — The Pemberton Vertical Light (2013)

A pair of trail runners witnessed a vertical column of light appear between two firs at dusk. It pulsed three times, then snapped out.

Case File 23L — The Coquihalla Red Drifter (2019)

Truckers repeatedly reported a red sphere drifting above the tree line around 3 a.m., moving parallel to the highway for kilometres before shooting straight up.

These lights often appear in places associated with:

- electrical anomalies

- Indigenous spirit warnings

- SAR vanishings

- ancient trails

CASE FILE CATEGORY V — FOREST WHISPERS & THE UNSEEN

The Ones You Don't See, But Feel

Sometimes nothing is seen or heard — but the *presence* is undeniable.

Case File 23M — The Okanagan Ridge Pressure (2020)

A jogger running a remote ridge felt a sudden weight in the air, like being stared at by multiple people. He turned and saw nothing — but the pressure persisted until he descended 300 metres.

Case File 23N — The Kootenay Camp Paralysis (2018)

A solo camper woke to the sensation of something inches from his tent. No footsteps, no breathing — just the thick presence of something waiting. He described it as "being observed by the valley itself."

Case File 23O — The North Island Tree-Line Shift (2012)

A wildlife technician scanning a hillside watched the shadows shift as if a tall figure stepped between them — without any visible form or movement.

WHAT THESE CASES TELL US

Every one of these encounters is different.But together, they reveal something simple:

The unexplained in British Columbia is not rare.It is constant.It is woven into the land.

People don't just report strange creatures.They report strange *moments*.

Moments where the forest feels aware.Moments where the coastline feels haunted.Moments where sound behaves wrong.Moments where time behaves wrong.Moments where something unseen steps alongside you.

BC is vast, raw, ancient, and layered with thousands of years of human experience — Indigenous, frontier, modern.

And in all that time, one truth remains:

There are parts of this province that do not reveal their secrets.They simply let you feel their presence and carry that memory home.

CHAPTER 24 — UFOS OF BRITISH COLUMBIA

Lights Over Lakes, Silent Craft in Mountain Passes & Encounters That Refuse Explanation

British Columbia is a place where the sky feels close.The mountains lift you into it.The sea reflects it back at you.And on clear nights, especially in the Interior, the stars look close enough to scoop with a hand.

It makes sense that UFO sightings have always been part of BC's wilderness history. What surprises people is just **how many** reports exist — and how long they've been documented.

From the Okanagan Valley to Vancouver Island, from the Nass River to the rugged passes around Smithers, thousands of witnesses have seen things that don't fit aircraft, satellites, meteors, drones, or atmospheric conditions.

Pilots.RCMP officers.Fishermen.Forestry workers.Loggers.Highway drivers.Campers.Entire families on their front decks at dusk.

This chapter explores the most compelling UFO encounters in British Columbia's history — not wild speculation, not conspiracies, but the grounded, bewildered accounts of regular people who saw something impossible in the sky.

BC's skies aren't just beautiful.They're active.

THE OKANAGAN VALLEY FLAPS

BC's UFO Hotspot With Decades of Activity

If one region of BC deserves the title of "UFO Central," it's the Okanagan Valley. For reasons no one can explain, this long corridor of mountains, orchards, lakes, and desert-like terrain has hosted multiple waves of sightings since at least the 1960s.

The 1968 Okanagan Flap

Multiple towns — Vernon, Peachland, Summerland, Penticton — reported the same thing:

- bright white spheres

- silent flight

- sudden accelerations

- hovering over Okanagan Lake

Witnesses included:

- a retired Air Force mechanic

- a doctor driving home from the hospital

- a group of orchard workers

- a pair of RCMP officers

The sightings came in waves for weeks. One officer described the object as:

"Too fast to be anything we knew.Too controlled to be a meteor.Too silent to be an aircraft."

The Kelowna Triangle Lights (1998–2005)

Dozens of reports describe:

- orange-red triangles

- hovering for minutes

- rotating slowly, silently

- then shooting upward at impossible speed

One family watched a triangular formation hover over Okanagan Mountain Park for nearly two minutes before it blinked out like a dying ember.

Modern Okanagan Encounters (2010–2023)

Witnesses continue to report:

- spinning disc-shaped lights

- glowing spheres rising from Okanagan Lake

- silent craft drifting between mountain ridges

- pulsating white lights hovering over vineyards

The number of independent witnesses makes the Okanagan one of Canada's most active UFO corridors.

THE VANCOUVER ISLAND SIGHTINGS

Coastal Craft, Silent Triangles & Lights Over the Pacific

Vancouver Island's west coast is brutal, raw, and largely uninhabited — perfect for unusual aerial phenomena.

The Alberni Inlet Craft (1972)

A famously credible case. A logging crew saw a metallic disc hover silently over the inlet, tilt, and shoot straight up. No sound. No wind. No contrails.

The Comox Triangle (1980s)

Radar technicians at CFB Comox tracked triangular craft performing maneuvers no jet could replicate. Multiple witnesses saw lights in a triangular formation shimmering over the Strait of Georgia.

The Tofino–Ucluelet Silent Visitor (2002)

Surfers on Long Beach saw a massive dark shape block stars overhead — a silent craft gliding north along the surfline, no lights, no sound, moving far too slowly to stay airborne.

One witness said:

"It felt like a shadow that shouldn't have been there."

Port Hardy Coastal Lights (2015–Present)

Dozens of fishermen and First Nations boaters have reported:

- orbs rising from the ocean

- lights pacing boats at night

- silent discs drifting low over inlets

- bright objects entering fog banks without reflection

These sightings often occur where cell service dies and the coastline turns primordial.

NORTHERN BC — THE HIGH STRANGENESS CORRIDOR

Prince George, Smithers, Terrace & Beyond

The farther north you go, the weirder the sky becomes.

The Terrace Lights (1960s–Present)

Terrace is famous for its mountain lights — white, blue, or orange spheres that drift between ridges, hover over valleys, or pulse above the Skeena River.

Many sightings are:

- low

- slow

- silent

- below cloud level

Geologists once speculated "earth lights" or magnetic anomalies. But the intelligence-like movements described by witnesses suggest more than natural activity.

The Smithers Valley Flash (1981)

RCMP officers and dozens of residents saw a brilliant oval-shaped craft explode into view over Hudson Bay Mountain, then drift slowly east before vanishing. No aircraft reported in the region.

The Prince George Cylinder (2010)

A long, metallic cylinder with no lights was seen drifting silently across Highway 97 at dusk. Three separate motorists reported the same shape and direction.

Nass Valley "Sky Walkers" (1990s)

Nisga'a residents reported tall glowing figures moving along ridgelines. Some believe these are sky spirits, not craft. Others insist they are connected to UFO phenomena.

THE EAST KOOTENAY FLYOVERS

Gold Mines, Mountain Valleys & Repeating Events

The Kootenays have long been a quiet hotspot.

The Kimberley Mine Lights (1960s)

Miners repeatedly saw:

- glowing orbs descending into the treeline

- silent disc shapes rising from behind tailing piles

Some joked the craft were "checking the ore quality."

The Cranbrook Barrel (1993)

Two hunters saw a barrel-shaped craft silently cruise over a valley, low enough to illuminate the trees beneath.

The Nelson Triangle (2005)

A silent triangle with three orange lights hovered for nearly 45 seconds over an alpine ridge before accelerating straight upward.

COASTAL HAUNTINGS OR UFOs? BOTH.

The Confusing Overlap of Supernatural Traditions & Modern Sightings

Indigenous sky-spirit stories across BC describe:

- glowing beings descending from clouds

- lights traveling up rivers

- bright orbs hovering above longhouses

- "flying canoes" carrying ancestors

Many Elders today acknowledge that some modern UFO sightings mirror ancient teachings — though they emphasize that these stories are spiritual traditions, not literal descriptions of craft.

Still, the parallels are striking.

PILOT REPORTS — THE MOST CREDIBLE WITNESSES

Bush pilots, commercial pilots, float-plane operators — BC's skies are full of them. And many have seen things they can't explain.

Case: The Vancouver–Nanaimo Blip (1983)

A commercial pilot saw a bright sphere pacing his aircraft at a fixed distance. It disappeared in a vertical climb.

Case: The Prince Rupert Twin-Lake Incident (1999)

A helicopter pilot saw two bright objects circle one another above a ridge — then merge into a single light.

Case: The Smithers Night Encounter (2017)

A pilot approaching Smithers saw three lights forming a triangle that rotated slowly, then blinked out as he descended.

Pilots rarely speak openly — but their reports are among the most consistent.

RURAL & BACKROAD ENCOUNTERS

Farmers, Loggers & People Who Know the Sky

BC's backroads generate some of the most detailed UFO encounters:

- silent craft hovering above clear-cuts

- orbs pacing logging trucks

- triangular formations following river valleys

- lights rising vertically from lakes

- hovering discs illuminating farm fields

One logger near Houston described a round craft the size of a pickup silently gliding between tree lines. He said:

"It moved like it wasn't part of this world."

CASE FILES — BC UFO ENCOUNTERS WITH NO EXPLANATION

Case File 24A — Okanagan Triple Sphere (1971)

Three glowing orbs hovered over Okanagan Lake for nearly a full minute. Witnesses across three towns reported the same event.

Case File 24B — Bamfield Silent Shadow (2002)

A massive triangular shadow passed over a surf campground. It blocked stars and made no sound.

Case File 24C — Terrace Ridge Pulse (2011)

A mountain-top glowing orb pulsed with rhythmic light for nearly ten minutes, witnessed by a Search & Rescue volunteer.

Case File 24D — Haida Gwaii Red Drop (2020)

A bright red sphere descended rapidly toward the water — then stopped centimetres above the ocean and hovered silently.

Case File 24E — Prince George Metallic Cylinder (2010)

A long cylinder drifted across the highway at dusk. No wings. No sound. Three drivers reported identical details.

WHAT DO THESE SIGHTINGS MEAN?

Theories fall into categories:

- **Classical UFO phenomena** – craft-like objects

- **Orb / earth-light phenomena** – natural but unexplained

- **Indigenous sky-spirit parallels** – cultural, spiritual interpretations

- **Military testing** – unlikely for silent, low-altitude craft

- **Atmospheric anomalies** – cannot explain intelligent motion

The truth is that BC's terrain — deep valleys, mountain passes, cold lakes, coastal fogbanks — creates perfect conditions for aerial phenomena, whatever their origin.

But one thing is clear:

BC's skies are not empty.Not by a long shot.

CHAPTER 25 — ORBS, MOUNTAIN LIGHTS & NIGHT GLOWS
The Silent Glimmers That Drift Through BC's Wildest Places

Before I ever studied UFO reports or dug into historical cases, I heard about **the lights**.

Not craft.Not ships.Not anything metallic or mechanical.

Just *lights* — drifting, pulsing, hovering, sliding between trees, floating above ridgelines, glowing like lanterns without a source.

Ask enough people across British Columbia and you'll realize something quickly:

BC's orb phenomenon is older, more widespread, and more consistent than its UFO sightings.

It happens in places with no cell service, no roads, no population — places where the forests breathe heavy and the nights fall like velvet.

Hunters talk about them.Hikers whisper about them.Indigenous Elders speak of them carefully.And Search & Rescue teams quietly admit they've seen more than they can explain.

This chapter dives into the strange lights that have haunted BC's wilderness for decades — maybe centuries.

THE TERRACE MOUNTAIN LIGHTS

A Mystery That Refuses to Fade

If you ask anyone in Terrace about the mountain lights, you won't get skepticism — you'll get stories. The phenomenon is so common that many locals simply shrug and say:

"Yeah, you'll see them eventually."

And they do.

Common Descriptions Include:

- glowing white or orange orbs

- floating just above treeline

- no flicker, no beam, no directional source

- moving horizontally, not downward like flares

- sometimes splitting into two or merging into one

Witnesses include:

- RCMP officers

- paramedics

- SAR members

- night-shift industrial workers

- hikers camping along the Skeena

These lights don't behave like aircraft or drones — they drift, hover, pulse, then fade as if absorbed by the mountains themselves.

Some nights, multiple orbs appear along the ridges like lanterns carried by invisible hands.

HAIDA GWAII — GLOWS OVER THE TREES

The Islands Where Earth, Water & Sky Blend Into One

Haida Gwaii has some of the oldest supernatural traditions on the coast — and the glowing lights reported here feel like a continuation of those ancient narratives.

Witnesses report:

- soft green or blue lights drifting above moss forests

- glowing shapes rising from beaches at night

- spheres floating over logging roads

- shimmering lights appearing above bogs or lakes

A fisherman once described a blue-white orb that hovered above the surf for so long he finished cleaning his catch before it finally winked out.

An Elder from Skidegate said:

"They're not visitors.They're reminders."

When asked what that meant, he shrugged:

"The land shows itself when it wants to."

THE FRASER CANYON NIGHT PULSE

A Mysterious Vertical Beam Seen by Dozens

Between Yale and Lytton, there have been reports spanning decades of a strange vertical beam of white or pale-yellow light appearing in narrow side valleys.

It is described as:

- a straight column, like a spotlight

- but with no source

- appearing in forested areas with no infrastructure

- lasting mere seconds before vanishing

One highway driver saw the beam descend from nowhere, hit the valley floor like a silent lightning bolt, and then vanish without a trace.

Forestry workers once stopped their trucks after witnessing a beam so bright it lit up an entire slope, even though no towns or equipment existed nearby.

This "pulse light" doesn't behave like lightning or headlights — it appears too localized, too vertical, and too controlled.

VANCOUVER ISLAND — ORBS IN THE OLD GROWTH

Lights That Wander Without Sound

Vancouver Island is one of the richest orb hotspots in Canada. Reports come from:

- Port Renfrew

- Cowichan Lake

- Strathcona backcountry

- Gold River valleys

- remote log roads near Woss

Witnesses describe:

- glowing spheres moving between massive cedar trunks

- orbs pacing hikers

- lights hovering above mossy riverbeds

- drifting gold or blue lights in fog

A forestry technician working alone saw a pale-white orb follow the logging road behind him at walking pace for nearly a kilometre — not speeding, not weaving, just silently keeping its distance.

He said:

"It felt like someone was carrying a light, but there was no one. No vehicle, no sound, nothing."

THE OKANAGAN VALLEY "GROUND LIGHTS"

Not in the Sky — On the Lakeshore

Unlike aerial UFOs, the Okanagan orb phenomenon is deeply tied to the land.

Witnesses have reported:

- orange lights moving along cliffs

- white orbs gliding above vineyards

- glowing shapes drifting across beaches at night

One of the strangest recurring sightings involves **orbs rising vertically from Okanagan Lake,** reaching 30–50 feet in height, then blinking out.

These events have been witnessed by:

- couples on evening walks

- fishermen

- lakefront residents

- tourists on balconies

The orbs make no sound and leave no reflection on the water — baffling observers who assume any light would disturb the surface.

THE INTERIOR VALLEY FLOATERS

Lights That Travel Ridgelines Like Beings on Patrol

From Merritt to Kamloops to the Cariboo, people have seen faint lights moving along mountaintops at night.

Some are described as:

- white or pale blue

- traveling horizontally

- maintaining consistent altitude

- moving at speeds too slow for aircraft but too smooth for people with headlamps

Ranchers in the Nicola Valley say the same thing:

"Those lights are older than us."

One ranch hand watched a light drift along a ridge, stop for a full minute, then continue on its way — as if someone paused to look down into the valley.

ARE THESE ATMOSPHERIC? NATURAL? SUPERNATURAL?

Scientists have offered theories:

- ball lightning

- swamp gas

- tectonic strain lights

- plasma

- reflections

- temperature inversion effects

But none of these fully match the intelligence-like movements described.

Indigenous interpretations often align more with land spirits or ancestral presences — lights that protect, warn, or communicate.

UFO researchers view them as possible probes or craft-related activity.

Wilderness veterans — loggers, hunters, SAR volunteers — often shrug and say:

"They're just part of BC."

The truth might be somewhere between all these explanations.

CASE FILES — MOUNTAIN LIGHTS & ORBS

Case File 25A — Terrace Ridge Lantern (1997)

A bright orange sphere hovered over a ridge for 20 minutes while dozens of locals watched. It moved slowly side to side, then faded like an ember.

Case File 25B — Haida Gwaii Forest Drift (2018)

A blue orb drifted between cedar trunks for several minutes, then vanished abruptly as if absorbed into the ground.

Case File 25C — Okanagan Lake Rising Orb (2004)

A glowing white sphere emerged from the lake surface at night, rose 40 feet, pulsed twice, then blinked out.

Case File 25D — Vancouver Island Moss Trail Light (2016)

A lone hiker saw a soft golden light pacing him for ten minutes, always staying 30 feet behind.

Case File 25E — Fraser Canyon Beam (2012)

A highway driver witnessed a vertical beam of white light strike a slope ahead. No infrastructure was present. No thunder. No sound.

WHAT THESE LIGHTS SUGGEST

Collectively, BC's lights share four key traits:

1. **Silent Movement**No hum, no wind, no engine noise.

2. **Intelligence-Like Behavior**They pace people, change direction, pause, merge, split.

3. **Connection to Wilderness Hotspots**They appear in places linked to:

- Sasquatch sightings

- disappearances

- haunted forests

- ancient Indigenous territory

- coastline spirit narratives

4. **Consistency Across Generations**1950 or 2024 — the descriptions match.

The lights may not be craft.They may not be spirits.They may not be atmospheric.They might be something that intersects all three — something older, deeper, woven into the land itself.

Whatever they are, one truth stands:

British Columbia shines in the dark — and not all those lights come from the stars.

CHAPTER 26 — CROSSOVERS: WHEN MYSTERIES OVERLAP
Bigfoot, Lights, Voices & the Valleys Where Boundaries Blur

Spend enough nights in British Columbia's wilderness and you begin noticing a pattern — not in the sightings themselves, but in where they happen. Certain valleys, certain mountain corridors, certain islands, certain deep pockets of forest... they don't just have *one* type of mystery.

They have *all of them.*

Sasquatch sightings.Orb lights.UFO craft.Mimicking voices.Phantom footsteps.Disappearances.Time slips.Shadow shapes.And sometimes, all in the same place — even the same night.

It is the overlap that raises eyebrows.It is the overlap that makes researchers stop and question what they thought they understood.And it is the overlap that suggests BC's deep wilderness might hold more than one mystery interacting in ways we don't yet comprehend.

This chapter explores those strange intersections — the crossroads of phenomena that should be separate but aren't.

THE "HOT VALLEYS" OF BRITISH COLUMBIA

Places Where Reports Cluster Together in Impossible Ways

Across BC, certain regions repeatedly produce multi-layered sightings:

- **Harrison Lake & Sasquatch Valley** — BC's Sasquatch capital also sees recurring orb lights, UFOs, and ridge-top glows.

- **Bella Coola & the Great Bear Rainforest** — creature sightings + lights + shadows that move with intelligence.

- **Terrace & the Skeena Corridor** — mountain lights + Sasquatch reports + unexplained footsteps.

- **Vancouver Island (North & West)** — strange orbs + creature encounters + mimicking voices in dense cedar groves.

- **Okanagan Valley** — UFO flaps + orbs rising from lakes + giant-figure sightings in high timber.

- **Fraser Canyon** — vertical light pulses + shadow watchers + roadside creatures.

When you map these reports geographically, they don't scatter randomly.They line up like beads on a thread.

The pattern suggests something important:

Certain landscapes act as amplifiers. Not for one phenomenon — but for many.

BIGFOOT + ORBS: A PATTERN TOO COMMON TO IGNORE

Creatures & Lights in the Same Forests, Often the Same Night

Across BC — and throughout North America — witnesses often describe glowing orbs in areas with active Sasquatch reports.

Examples include:

1. Harrison Lake Ridge (multiple years)

Hikers heard bipedal footsteps pacing them in brush. Twenty minutes later, a blue orb drifted between firs at chest height.

2. North Vancouver Island (2012)

A hunter saw a tall shadow move behind a cedar. Minutes later, a green-white orb appeared above the same spot and floated uphill silently.

3. Nisga'a Territory (1990s)

Residents reported giant figures on ridgelines followed by clusters of floating lights the same evening.

4. Nicola Valley (2005)

A rancher found large, barefoot tracks in new snow. That night, orange orbs hovered low over the same field.

Some researchers see this as coincidence.Others see a connection — not necessarily between the phenomena themselves, but between the conditions that *produce* them.

Dense forests.Rugged terrain.Deep isolation.Ancient Indigenous territory.Low human presence.High wildlife density.Strong river/valley systems.

And sometimes, high electromagnetic activity.

These environments may act as "windows" where unusual things cluster.

UFOs + BIGFOOT: THE CONTROVERSIAL CROSSOVER

Not Saying They're Related — But the Sightings Frequently Coincide

For decades, Bigfoot researchers avoided discussing UFOs to keep their work credible.UFO researchers avoided Bigfoot for the same reason.But BC doesn't care about the boundaries between fields.

It gives both.

Often in the same region.Occasionally in the same 24 hours.

Case: Mission, BC (1970s)

Residents saw a large, silent craft hover over the tree line. Two nights later, multiple families heard heavy bipedal footsteps outside cabins along Stave Lake.

Case: Bella Coola Backcountry (2000s)

Campers witnessed a low-floating disc with a blue light. Hours later, two of them heard guttural grunts and bipedal movement pacing the camp.

Case: North Okanagan (1981)

Bright white orbs hovered above a ridge. The next morning, hikers discovered large barefoot tracks in damp moss.

Are these related?Or do these valleys simply attract multiple forms of phenomenon because they're remote and unobserved?

Right now, no one knows.But the overlap is undeniable.

SHADOWS + LIGHTS + SOUNDS

When Terrains Behave Like They Have a Mind

Many BC wilderness zones exhibit multiple anomalies simultaneously:

- Shadow figures pacing treelines

- Orbs drifting along ridges

- Mimicking voices

- Footsteps with no source

- Sudden dead silence

- Strange lights in the sky

- Missing time events

Often during the same outing.

This isn't Bigfoot.This isn't UFOs.This isn't spirits.

It's the landscape itself producing multiple layers of strangeness — as if the valley is active, watching, interacting.

Search & Rescue volunteers sometimes describe valleys as "alive," "charged," or "off," especially during major missing-person cases.

One SAR member near Golden said:

"You can feel when a valley is wrong.It hits you before you even step out of the truck."

INDIGENOUS PERSPECTIVE — EVERYTHING IS CONNECTED

Indigenous Elders across BC rarely separate these events into categories.

To them, the land, sky, water, animals, ancestors, spirits, and unexplainable events form a single living system.

One Elder from the Interior said:

"When something changes in the sky, something else changes in the forest.Everything listens to everything."

Another from the coast explained:

"Lights, shadows, voices — they are not separate.The land has many layers. Sometimes you walk through more than one."

This worldview doesn't impose explanations; it simply acknowledges complexity.

And honestly? It makes more sense than anything the scientific or paranormal communities have offered.

THE TRIANGLE ZONES OF BC

Regions Where ALL Phenomena Overlap

There are a handful of places in BC where the three major categories — creatures, craft, and lights — occur repeatedly:

1. Harrison–Chehalis Triangle

- dozens of Sasquatch reports

- ridge orbs

- sky flaps

- mimicking voices

2. Bella Coola / Talchako Triangle

- shadow beings

- craft-like lights

- deep-forest activity

- orbs in cedar groves

3. Terrace–Nass Valley Corridor

- mountain lights

- stick structures

- large-figure sightings

- footsteps in moss

4. Vancouver Island North

- creature tracks

- orb activity

- mimics

- sky lights along the coast

These "triangles" are not arbitrary; they're mapped through decades of witness reports.

WHY DO THESE CROSSOVERS HAPPEN?

There are four major theories:

1. Shared Environmental Conditions

Remote valleys may create electromagnetic, atmospheric, or geological conditions that produce multiple anomalies.

2. Multiple Phenomena, Same Habitat

Sasquatch, natural earth lights, UFOs — all attracted to the same deep wilderness.

3. Human Perception Shifts

Extreme isolation and silence may heighten sensory awareness or trigger unusual perceptions.

4. A Single Underlying Source

The most controversial idea:that these events may be different manifestations of the same unknown process.

An Elder said it best:

"When the land wakes up, everything wakes with it."

CASE FILES — CROSSOVER INCIDENTS

Case File 26A — Bella Coola Triple Event (2014)

Campers saw a disc-shaped light, heard bipedal footsteps circling camp, and witnessed a glowing orb drifting through the trees.

Case File 26B — Harrison Ridge Sequence (1999)

Over three nights:

- loud whoops

- large tracks

- orange orbs drifting across lake

- a triangular formation hovering low in the valley

Case File 26C — Terrace Ridge Multi-Phenomena (2018)

A hunter saw a shadow figure at dusk, then a blue orb at treeline, followed by a silent object crossing the sky at low altitude.

Case File 26D — Gold River Mimic & Light (2012)

A mimic voice lured a hiker off trail. Minutes later, a white orb hovered near a cedar stand.

THE UNANSWERED QUESTION

Do these mysteries feed off one another?Are they unrelated events simply sharing the same stage?Or is BC a place where the boundary between the ordinary and the extraordinary thins?

Whatever the truth is, one thing is clear:

Where the phenomena overlap, the wilderness feels different.Charged.Aware.And watching.

In these valleys, you don't just observe the land —**the land observes you back.**

CHAPTER 27 — PHANTOM WOLVES, GIANT BIRDS & OTHER CREATURES

The Beasts That Haunt BC's Edges — From Thunderbirds to Shadow Wolves & Vanished Species That Shouldn't Be Here

British Columbia is known for its Sasquatch stories — the creature dominates nearly every conversation about wilderness mysteries. But what people forget is that BC's landscape holds *dozens* of creature legends and strange modern sightings that have nothing to do with Bigfoot at all.

Some are ancient.Some are recent.Some come from Indigenous cosmology.Some come from hunters, fishermen, truckers, or hikers.Some are tied to real species that once roamed here — wolves, great birds, predators that vanished long before modern settlement.

Others?They exist in that grey zone between myth and reality, where eyewitness testimony overlaps with old oral tradition and unexplained encounters.

This chapter explores those other beings — the ones that slip through forests silently, glide over mountain peaks with wings wider than a bush plane, or leave prints in mud that don't match any known species.

THE PHANTOM WOLVES OF BC

Oversized, Silent, and Seen in Regions Where No Such Wolves Should Exist

Wolves are not unusual in British Columbia — the province has healthy populations across the North, the Interior, and Vancouver Island. But Phantom Wolves are different.

People describe animals that:

- are far larger than normal

- move silently even in brush

- have darker, almost shadow-like fur

- appear suddenly, watching

- vanish between trees without noise

- leave no tracks

- or leave *massive* tracks inconsistent with known wolf species

Reports come from:

- the Nass Valley

- the Kootenays

- the Chilcotin Plateau

- northern Vancouver Island

- Bella Coola's deep valleys

- Haida Gwaii (rare but documented)

Common Traits in Sightings

1. **Size:** Witnesses describe wolves the size of ponies — 200 to 250 pounds, far larger than the average BC wolf.

2. **Gait:** Phantom Wolves move with unnatural quietness, even in dry branches or alder thickets.

3. **Eyes:** Some describe strange eye shine — not typical yellow or green, but pale blue, white, or even orange.

4. **Tracks:**When tracks are found, they are enormous — bigger than any timber wolf print on record.

5. **Behavior:**Phantom Wolves watch people. They don't flee.They stand still, observe, then fade away.

Are They Real Wolves?

Some wildlife experts suggest:

- relict populations of prehistoric wolves,

- unusually large individuals,

- crossbreeds with dogs or escaped exotics,

- or simply misjudgment of size.

But many sightings occur in places where distance and scale are easy to judge — alpine ridgelines, river flats, frozen lakes.

Hunters insist:

"That wasn't a wolf.That was something else."

Indigenous teachings describe giant wolves that act as protectors or omens — beings tied to the land, not simply animals.And modern sightings align with these stories shockingly well.

THE SEA-WOLVES OF COASTAL BC

A Real Species With Myth-Like Behavior

Unlike Phantom Wolves, **Sea-Wolves are real** — genetically distinct coastal wolves that fish, swim, travel beaches, and move across islands with ease.

But their behavior feels uncanny:

- they swim across open ocean

- they haul out on beaches like seals

- they hunt salmon, mussels, and seals

- they move with ghostlike silence

- they appear in regions associated with supernatural sea-beings

Fishermen sometimes report seeing wolves swimming between islands at dawn, their heads cutting the water like dark spirits.

In Heiltsuk and Wuikinuxv territories, wolves have spiritual significance — often seen as guides, protectors, or omens. When you see a Sea-Wolf in fog or moonlight, you understand why.

THE GIANT BIRDS OF BRITISH COLUMBIA

Thunderbirds, Sky Predators & Birds Larger Than Any Known Species

BC's Thunderbird legends are widely known, but what surprises people is that *modern sightings still happen.*

Not often — but enough to form a pattern.

Witnesses across BC describe:

- massive dark birds

- wingspans between 12 and 20 feet

- slow, powerful wingbeats

- silent gliding

- perched shapes on cliffs that vanish on approach

Where These Sightings Occur

- the Fraser Canyon

- the Chilcotin Plateau

- Bella Coola's glacier valleys

- the Stikine region

- Vancouver Island mountains

- the Kootenay backcountry

- Haida Gwaii cliffs

Common Details

1. **Huge Wingspans:**Often compared to small planes or gliders.

2. **Feathered, Not Pterosaur-like:**Most witnesses insist the animals look like real birds — just impossibly large.

3. **Silent Flight:**No sound, no turbulence, no wing noise.

4. **Perching on Sheer Cliffs:**Some sightings involve birds perched in places unreachable by anything but a raptor.

Possible Explanations

- misidentified eagles?Unlikely — size descriptions are too extreme.

- surviving Terratorns?An extinct giant bird, once native to North America.

- spirit beings from Indigenous tradition?Thunderbirds are often described as sky protectors or storm-bringers.

One pilot near Terrace reported:

"It passed under me.Wings the size of a float plane.I'll never forget it."

These sightings are rare — but persistent.

THE PALE PREDATORS

White or Grey Animals Too Large to Identify

Another class of creature sighting involves large, pale predators — often described as:

- massive

- white or light grey

- wolf-like but bigger

- cougar-like but bulkier

- silent

- appearing in fog, snowstorms, or dusk

Sightings occur mostly in:

- northern BC

- Haida Gwaii

- the Yukon border

- the Stewart–Cassiar corridor

One trapper near Dease Lake described a pale beast as:

"A wolf the size of a cow moose, but not shaped like any wolf I've ever seen."

These animals move with eerie smoothness and often vanish into forests where tracks mysteriously fail to appear.

THE RAVEN PEOPLE & SHAPESHIFTERS

Supernatural beings that overlap with real animals

Across BC, ravens hold deep spiritual significance.Some teachings say ravens can shift between forms — human, spirit, animal — appearing in moments of transition.

Modern hikers report:

- ravens appearing repeatedly on multi-day trips

- unusually large ravens watching silently

- ravens flying patterns around hikers

- ravens appearing just before or after strange events

Some hikers claim ravens led them out of confusing terrain.Others say ravens watched them until they left a valley that "felt wrong."

These stories line up with teachings that ravens act as:

- guides

- warners

- protectors

- tricksters

Not creatures in the biological sense — but beings that connect the land's consciousness to the physical world.

THE "SHADOW BEASTS" OF BC

Creatures Without Detail — Only Shape

A handful of hikers and hunters report seeing large, animal-like shapes that:

- lack definition

- appear black or dark grey

- move like animals

- disappear instantly

- leave no tracks

They are often seen in:

- fog

- rain

- twilight

- deep moss forests

- cedar swamps

Witnesses feel a cold rush or sense of wrongness after the sighting — suggesting these might be perceptual experiences tied to dangerous terrain.

Or something older.

CASE FILES — OTHER CREATURES OF BC

Case File 29A — The Chilcotin Ridge Giant (2007)

A rancher saw a massive bird glide across a meadow, wings as wide as a pickup truck. No sound. No feathers found.

Case File 29B — The Nass Phantom Wolf (2014)

Three hunters watched a wolf the size of a pony cross a river. It left no tracks on the far bank.

Case File 29C — The Haida Gwaii Fog Predator (2019)

A pale, enormous animal stalked the edge of a logging road in thick fog. It vanished without sound.

Case File 29D — The Fraser Canyon Sky Shape (1998)

Motorists saw a giant bird-like silhouette pass over Highway 1. No aircraft were reported.

Case File 29E — North Island Shadow Wolf (2011)

A hiker observed a massive dark wolf pacing the treeline. It disappeared when he blinked.

WHAT THESE CREATURES MEAN

Not every creature sighting can be explained biologically.Not every legend is literal.Not every eyewitness report is accurate.

But when enough people across enough decades describe:

- wolves too large to be wolves

- birds too large to be birds

- pale predators

- shadow beasts

- supernatural guardians

you begin to see a pattern:

BC's wilderness isn't just home to creatures we know —it may be home to creatures we've forgotten, or creatures that exist in the space between worlds.

Whether physical, spiritual, or psychological, these beings leave the same impression:

Something else walks these forests.Something else flies above these mountains.Something else lives here with us.

And like everything else in British Columbia's wilderness,it keeps its distance —but never fully leaves our world behind.

EPILOGUE — WHAT THE WILDERNESS TEACHES US
In the End, It Isn't About Proof. It's About Paying Attention.

If there's one thing British Columbia teaches you — whether you come here as a researcher, a hiker, a believer, or just someone curious about the unexplained — it's this:

The wilderness doesn't owe you answers.But it will give you moments.

Moments that stay with you.Moments you think about years later.Moments that remind you the world is far stranger than we pretend it is.

I've spent years in forests across Canada, especially back home in Ontario. But BC feels different. It feels *older*. Wilder. Less filtered by the human hand. Walk far enough into its mountains or drift deep enough into its inlets and you feel yourself getting smaller in the best possible way.

These stories — Bigfoot encounters, strange lights, phantom wolves, voices in the trees, sky glows, haunted waters — they aren't just campfire tales. They're a record of what people experience when they let themselves step beyond the edges of the map and see the land for what it is:

Alive. Ancient. Aware.

And that's something you notice early on in this work:Not every sighting is a creature.Not every light is a craft.Not every voice is a spirit.Not every shadow is a watcher.

But sometimes they are.

And even when they're not, they still teach you something.They teach you to listen harder.To trust your instincts.To be humble out there.To understand that not every valley is for you. And that sometimes, the best you can do is acknowledge the mystery and leave it be.

I've learned that most people don't go into the wilderness looking for the strange. It finds them. On a quiet trail. On a foggy ridge. At a lonely lake. From the edge of a firelight. Or during a moment when they stop to breathe and realize the forest has gone silent around them.

The truth is, we don't have to solve these mysteries. We don't have to capture perfect evidence or come home with something the world cannot deny. We don't have to prove every creature or phenomenon that's been whispered about for centuries.

What we *can* do — what matters — is simply this:

Pay attention. Respect the land. Share what you've seen. And keep the door to the unknown open.

Because the moment we decide we already know everything, the wilderness stops teaching us. And no one wants that.

British Columbia remains one of the last true frontiers on the continent. Not because of its size or remoteness, but because it's a place where mystery still lives in broad daylight. Where the old stories still walk among the trees. Where the land hasn't forgotten anything — not the beings who came before, not the warnings, not the watchers, not the lights that drift through its mountains.

You leave BC changed. You leave it carrying more wonder than you arrived with. You leave knowing the world is far bigger, stranger, and deeper than anyone can fit between book covers.

And if you're lucky, you leave wanting to go back — not for answers, but for the feeling of standing once again on the edge of something vast and alive.

In the end, that's what every mystery leaves you with:**the understanding that the wilderness doesn't hide anything.It simply waits for you to notice.**

And if you're quiet, patient, and respectful…sometimes it lets you see a little more than you expect.

— Timothy D

APPENDIX A — BRITISH COLUMBIA BIGFOOT SIGHTINGS DATABASE (EXPANDED)

Note to the reader: This appendix is *not* a complete record of every Sasquatch report in British Columbia. It's a working field list, built from public databases (BFRO, Squatchable, historic John Green material), Sasquatch Canada–type archives, media coverage, and personal accounts.

Many encounters remain unreported. Others are still under investigation or are held back by witnesses, local researchers, or Indigenous communities who choose not to share them publicly. This database is meant as **a starting map**, not the whole territory.

I've grouped reports by region and given short "case file"–style entries rather than full narratives. In the main chapters, only a fraction of these make it into the storytelling. Here you get the wider backbone of BC's Sasquatch history.

1. VANCOUVER ISLAND & COASTAL ISLANDS

A mix of historic reports, modern encounters, and ongoing activity. Vancouver Island, Cormorant Island, and the nearby channels remain some of BC's highest-potential areas.

- **Early 1900s – Vancouver Island (Cowichan area)**Newspaper mentions of "wild man" and strange cries in the Cowichan region, including a 1905 reference to foul odour associated with a "hairy giant."

- **May 1974 – Shawnigan Lake (Class A)**Woman recalls multiple-witness daylight sighting of a large, hair-covered figure near the shore. Later archived in BFRO as a key historic Island case.

- **1960s–1970s – "Valdez/Alert Bay Wildman" Tradition**Accounts of wildman encounters on an island off the north tip of Vancouver Island (in the vicinity of Cormorant Island/Alert Bay), preserved in cryptozoological writeups and more recent retrospectives.

- **1990s–Present – Cowichan Lake & River Area (Multiple Class A/B)**Repeated reports of large tracks, nocturnal howls, and close-range sightings in forested slopes and river corridors near Cowichan Lake. BFRO lists several incidents, including early-morning sightings and vocalizations.

- **June 2006 – Cowichan Lake Vicinity (Class A)**Early-morning sighting on Vancouver Island near Cowichan Lake; witness observes a tall, upright figure moving through cutblock edge at close range.

- **October 2005 – South Island (Duncan area, Class A/B)**Sequence of incidents near a suspected "nest" site on Vancouver Island: possible lair-like ground structure, recurring nocturnal vocalizations, and one brief visual.

- **2014 – Clayoquot Sound, Remote Cabin Encounter (Narrative Account)**Solo paddler and photographer Sander Jain reports a prolonged, unnerving encounter at a hidden cabin in Clayoquot Sound: heavy bipedal footsteps, intimidation behaviour, and the sense of a huge presence circling the cabin at night. Later published as a detailed first-person account.

- **2010s–Present – Nahmint Valley & Remote West Coast Inlets**Ongoing claims from kayakers, small-boat operators, and backroad loggers of howls, rock-throwing, and possible large tracks along valley bottoms and spurs, sometimes featured in online expedition content and interviews.

- **2015–2023 – Cormorant Island / Alert Bay (Vocalizations & Possible Sightings)**Residents report bizarre, powerful howls coming from the forest behind Alert Bay; media coverage notes locals suspect Sasquatch, and follow-up articles describe a long history of Sasquatch lore and sightings on and near Cormorant Island.

- **2010s–2020s – North Vancouver Island General Region**Individual reports from hikers and locals describing tall, dark figures crossing logging roads, tree-knock sounds, and powerful vocalizations in valleys reachable only by long gravel access, mentioned in personal blogs and anecdotal accounts.

2. HARRISON LAKE, FRASER VALLEY & SOUTH COAST

One of the most famous Sasquatch hotspots in the world, with some of the longest-running databases thanks to researchers like John Green.

- **Late 1800s–Early 1900s – Harrison & Chehalis Traditions**Local and settler reports of "hairy giants" in the Harrison–Chehalis corridor, later compiled by John Green and other early researchers.

- **1960s–1990s – Multiple Harrison Lake Sightings**Campers, hunters, and boaters report road crossings, slope-climbing figures, and nocturnal screams in the surrounding mountains; many of these events became foundational in BC Sasquatch literature.

- **February 1996 – North Harrison Lake (Class B)**Campers report possible stalking behaviour at the north end of Harrison

Lake: heavy bipedal movement around camp, sticks snapping, and a sense of being watched.

- **September 2016 – Harrison Lake Area (Class A)**Swedish archaeologist on a BFRO expedition has a clear daylight sighting of a large, upright figure on a slope near Harrison Lake—considered one of the better modern "expedition" visuals in BC.

- **2000s–2010s – Chilliwack Lake & Skagit Valley (Class A/ B)**Multiple cases: rock-throwing at campers, possible track finds, and a Class B report of snow tracks in Skagit Valley, as well as vocalizations heard deep in Chilliwack Lake Provincial Park.

- **2005 – Othello Road Near Hope (Class A)**Trucker reports an early-morning roadside Sasquatch crossing; one of several "Coquihalla / canyon" type road incidents logged in databases.

3. OKANAGAN, THOMPSON & SOUTHERN INTERIOR

Better known in pop culture for Ogopogo and UFOs—but Sasquatch reports are steady here too.

- **Early 1950s – Between Peachland & Princeton**Logging camp cook encounters a large, hair-covered figure near camp while workers are away—an early Interior case still cited in summary lists.

- **1990s–2000s – Lumby & Shuswap Region (Class B)**Several reports of prolonged eerie screams near Lumby, possible track finds, and nocturnal vocal activity noted in small lakes and backroads east of the Okanagan.

- **September 2000s – BC Interior "Footprints Found" (Class B)**Hikers and hunters report large barefoot tracks in mud and soft soil in remote Interior valleys, often logged as secondary Class B cases in databases.

- **February 2018 – Heffley Lake Outside Kamloops (Class B)**Late-night road crossing: driver reports a large bipedal figure crossing ahead of vehicle, with a brief but clear silhouette against snow.

- **Similkameen River – South Okanagan Valley (Class A, Early 2000s)**A BC family watches what appears to be a **group of four Sasquatch** moving along a river section for several minutes; later documented as a family-group sighting, unusual for the number of subjects observed.

4. KOOTENAYS & COLUMBIA MOUNTAINS

Steep terrain, deep valleys, old mining towns, and a long record of wilderness encounters.

- **November 1995 – Ainsworth Hot Springs (Class A)**Motorist sees an 8-foot-tall creature crossing the road near Ainsworth Hot Springs at night; one of the better-known Kootenay road encounters.

- **1990s – Nakusp Region (Class A/B)**Swimmers and campers near Nakusp report distant vocalizations followed by possible tracks found the next day.

- **Various Dates – Kootenay Lakes & Side Valleys**Multi-decade pattern of sightings, screams, and track finds along Kootenay Lake, small upland lakes, and remote forestry roads; some cases extend from 1970 to present in personal collections.

5. NORTHERN BC, NASS & SKEENA CORRIDORS

Wild, low-density country with a combination of Indigenous lore and modern road sightings.

- **January 1996 – Southeast of McBride (Class B)**Large tracks found in snow near a residence in a remote area; tracks show long stride and barefoot impressions.

- **September 2000s – Muskwa River Floodplain (Class B)**Man finds large, human-like tracks in mud on Muskwa River flats, in extremely remote country; later logged as a northern BC Class B.

- **August 2019 – Just South of Nass River Bridge (Class A)**RV motorist gets a clear **daylight** sighting of a large, upright, hair-covered figure on Highway 37 south of the Nass River Bridge; considered one of the stronger recent northern Class A cases.

- **Nass River Valley – Ongoing Stories**Repeated mentions in personal accounts and informal discussions of Sasquatch activity in the Nass Valley region, sometimes woven into "Headless Valley"–style lore and other wilderness-strangeness narratives.

- **Dawson Creek Area – Possible Nest (Class B)**Report of a large ground structure interpreted by some investigators as a possible Sasquatch nest, along with incidental activity in surrounding cutblocks.

6. CENTRAL & NORTH COAST (BELLA COOLA, PRINCESS ROYAL, ETC.)

These are some of the most remote and dramatic landscapes in BC — and they have the stories to match.

- **Mid–Princess Royal Island, Fall 1995 (Class C / Summary)**Mentioned in summary DBs as a creature hiding behind a large boulder; this island and surrounding coast are often cited as prime "if they exist, they're here" Sasquatch habitat.

- **Bella Coola Region – Multiple Accounts (20th Century–Present)**Various encounters gathered by researchers interviewing Nuxalk and local residents: large bipedal figures on riverbars, unsettling vocalizations, and track finds in valleys only accessible by boat or single access road.

7. INTERIOR PLATEAUS & OTHER KEY CASES

A catch-all for notable reports that don't sit neatly in one valley system.

- **Read Island – 1996 (Class B)**Mother and child hear a powerful roar while lost in the forest on Read Island (between Vancouver Island and the mainland), later interpreted as possible Sasquatch vocalization.

- **Forest Technician Helicopter-Only Area (1993, Class B)**A forest service technician finds tracks in snow in a region so remote it is reachable only by helicopter; logged as one of the more interesting "no human access" footprint cases.

- **Snow Tracks in Skagit / Cascades (Spring 2000, Class B)**Possible snow tracks discovered in a rugged valley near the US border; photos later archived online and in BFRO records.

8. MODERN DATABASES & OVERALL NUMBERS

While John Green's historical files and the BFRO's geographical database remain the backbone of public BC Sasquatch records, several newer resources exist:

- **BFRO BC Geographical Database**Lists over a hundred British Columbia reports (Class A–C), ranging from 1800s narratives to 2020s road sightings and expedition results.

- **Online Sightings Maps (BC/NWT/Yukon)**Independent mappers have compiled Google Earth–style overlays with pins for virtually all documented BC reports, linking back to primary sources (BFRO, books, articles).

- **"Best Odds to Spot Bigfoot" Analyses (Media)**Several recent data-driven articles, based primarily on BFRO numbers, place British Columbia as **the top Canadian province** for Bigfoot sightings, with roughly 130–135 catalogued encounters and very high forest coverage.

- **BC Government Environmental Note (Bindernagel Reference)**A 2009 BC Ministry document on the "elusive Sasquatch" acknowledges Bindernagel's work and notes that sightings have been reported near Harrison Lake, Bradley Lagoon, Cranbrook, Fruitvale, and other regions—effectively admitting the pattern exists even while remaining noncommittal on the animal's reality.

HOW TO USE THIS APPENDIX IN THE FIELD

This database is deliberately **broad, not exhaustive**. It's meant to:

- show **where** patterns cluster

- help you choose research zones

- provide **historic context** for modern encounters

- remind you that if you're in any of these valleys, **you are not the first one there** wondering what walks the ridgelines

If you're heading into any of the areas listed:

- Mark the **historic incidents** on a map.

- Look for **corridors**: rivers, old game trails, logging roads that tie encounters together.

- Cross-reference with **orb lights, vanishings, and Indigenous lore** in earlier chapters of this book.

- And remember: **the best data you'll ever add to this database is your own careful, honest field notes.**

In the end, this appendix is a snapshot.

The real database is out there, in the mountains and valleys of BC, still walking, still leaving prints in places most people never go.

APPENDIX B — LAKE MONSTER SIGHTINGS INDEX (BRITISH COLUMBIA)

Note to the reader: This is a **working index**, not a complete catalogue of every lake-monster story in British Columbia. A lot of the best material lives in private files, out-of-print books, newsrooms, and people's memories. Some lakes have strong traditions but only a handful of written reports. Others likely have stories that were never recorded at all.

Think of this as a **field-use overview**: the main lakes, the main monsters, and the key cases you can trace back if you want to dig deeper.

I've grouped things by lake or region, with short case-style entries rather than full narratives. Ogopogo and Shuswaggi get the most space, because they're where most of the data is. A final section lists "other candidates" — lakes that show up in research papers and regional lore as possible monster habitats.

1. OKANAGAN LAKE — OGOPOGO / N̓X̌AʔX̌ʔITKʷ

British Columbia's most famous lake monster. Indigenous stories long predate the "Ogopogo" name, describing a powerful water spirit or entity associated with Okanagan Lake and its narrows. Modern sightings start in the late 1800s and continue well into the 2020s.

Key early accounts

- **Pre-contact – Syilx / Okanagan traditions**Stories of N̓xaʔx̌ʔitkʷ ("lake demon" or spirit) tied to the narrows near present-day Rattlesnake Island, where offerings were made before crossings. The being is powerful, dangerous, and tied to the spirit of the water, not just a "creature."

- **1872–1873 – Susan Allison sighting**One of the earliest written settler reports: Allison describes a long, serpentine animal near her ranch shoreline (modern West Kelowna). Her description closely matches Indigenous accounts of a multi-humped, serpentine form.

- **1926 – Okanagan Mission / "Thirty cars" incident (multi-witness)**Occupants of roughly 30 cars parked along the shore observe a large, multi-humped creature moving out in the lake, "like several logs in a line." This mass sighting later becomes one of the cornerstone cases in Ogopogo literature.

- **1947 – Multi-boat encounter**Several boaters report seeing a 30-foot multi-humped creature with what one witness describes as a forked tail and undulating humps. The description is detailed enough to be quoted repeatedly in later books and articles.

Mid-20th century clusters

- **1950s–1970s – Repeated hump and wake sightings**Numerous smaller cases: fishermen, pleasure boaters, and lakeshore residents report long lines of humps, unexplained wakes on calm water, and "something like a huge log suddenly moving under its own power."

- **1960s–1980s – "Head and neck" reports**A minority of witnesses describe a head and neck rising above the surface, often horse-like or reptilian. Some of these become the basis of later illustrations and marketing.

Late 20th century to early 2000s

- **1980s–1990s – Photograph and film era**Several still photos and a few film/video clips emerge. Quality varies, but a handful of frames continue to be cited as some of the strongest visual evidence: multi-humped wakes, dark forms, and at least one possible "head" image.

- **Ongoing dive stories**Divers working near the floating bridge and deep moorings report unnerving encounters: massive shapes in the gloom, a single large "eye" in their light beam, and the sense that something big moved just out of view. These are mostly anecdotal, but they persist in local talk.

Recent decades

- **2015 – "Head" photo (Kelowna area)**A Kelowna man, Bill Steciuk, captures an image he believes shows Ogopogo's head, shared in local and national media; he maintains a long-running sightings log and notes that late August–early October is peak season for reports.

- **2018 – Two more reported sightings near Kelowna**Steciuk reports fresh visuals, arguing that patterns of movement and wake suggest a large animal rather than boat wake or logs. These help reignite interest in the legend.

- **2022 – Viral "head at the surface" photo**A photograph circulates online appearing to show a dark head or object protruding from calm Okanagan Lake. Coverage frames it as another in a long line of "maybe Ogopogo" images, reinforcing how active the legend still is.

- **2025 – Ongoing shoreline images and phone videos**Local media and social channels continue to feature periodic clips of odd wakes, distant humps, and unexplained surface disturbances — rarely conclusive, but enough to keep the legend very much alive.

2. SHUSWAP LAKE — SHUSWAGGI / SICÓPOGO / TA-ZUM-A

Shuswap Lake's monster has worn several names over the years: **Shuswaggi**, **Sicopogo**, and Ta-Zum-A among them. The lake has fewer people on its shoreline than Okanagan, which probably explains the lower number of written reports—but the quality of some cases is surprisingly strong.

Early mentions

- **c. 1904 – Early written references**Local news and oral recollections refer to an unknown creature in Shuswap Lake, sometimes compared to a giant eel or serpentine animal rising in sections from the water.

- **1948 – Mr. Dew's upended boat (key classic case)**While out on the lake, a Mr. Dew reports something large coming towards his boat underwater, churning the water enough to nearly flip the vessel. The creature passes underneath and surfaces on the far side, described as a long-necked animal with substantial mass.

- **1948 (second case, same year)**Another sighting with similar description — long body, visible mass moving under the water — raises questions about whether a specific animal was active near the surface that season.

- **1970 – Family birthday sighting**A family celebrating a birthday on or near the lake spots what they describe as a strange multi-humped animal at a distance, moving steadily before submerging. Details vary, but the impression is of something large, animate, and unlike typical boat wake or fish.

1980s–2000s

- **1980s – Linda Griffiths binocular encounter**While viewing the lake through binoculars, Griffiths reports a long, serpent-like creature near a boat, estimating it at around eight metres (26 feet) in length with multiple humps. Her description is often cited as one of the clearest Shuswaggi observations.

- **Various dates – Sturgeon vs monster question**Locals note the presence of large sturgeon in Shuswap Lake, but argue that sturgeon are bottom-feeding and rarely create the kind of multi-hump surface display associated with Shuswaggi.

Modern, filmed encounters

- **March 23, 2019 – Murdoch Point fishermen video**Two anglers filming an episode of *Two Guys With Flies* on Shuswap Lake capture unusual, repeating surface humps and wave patterns, accompanied by a loud "breach" sound like air or water being forced out at the surface. In the video, one of them labels it "the Shuswaggi." Global News later runs the story alongside a Skaha Ogopogo clip.

- **Summer 2023 – McRae family sighting & video**Less than a day into their stay at a Shuswap lakeside home, the family records video of large, organized ripples and what they describe as a series of grey humps about 150–300 metres away. While the footage itself is inconclusive, the first-hand account is enthusiastic and consistent with classic descriptions: organized humps, not random chop.

- **Ongoing 2020s – Letters and local commentary**Columns and letters-to-the-editor continue to revisit Shuswaggi, summarizing past cases and speculating on whether a real, unknown animal — possibly sturgeon, possibly something else — lies behind the pattern.

3. SKAHA, OSOYOOS & OTHER OKANAGAN-CHAIN LAKES

These lakes are physically linked to Okanagan Lake through rivers and channels, which has led to the idea that a single breeding population — whether real or folkloric — might move through the system. A more conservative explanation is that once people know Ogopogo is "nearby," they interpret odd wave events through that lens.

Skaha Lake

- **June 1, 2019 – Jim La Rocque Skaha video**On Skaha Lake near Kaleden, La Rocque films a long, moving disturbance with what he interprets as multiple "flippers" or humps creating a synchronized rolling motion. He estimates it at up to 120 feet long and calls it "definitive Ogopogo evidence." Skeptics point out that classic Ogopogo is associated with Okanagan Lake proper, but others note that the chain is hydrologically connected.

Osoyoos Lake

- **Historic and modern reports (summary)**Research pieces and anomalistics papers list Osoyoos among BC's "monster lakes," with suggestions that very large sturgeon and/or an Ogopogo-like serpent may account for surface anomalies. Specific cases are rarely detailed publicly but the lake appears in multiple compiled lists.

Other Interior lakes

A technical paper on Canadian lake-monster and anomalous-animal reports lists several other BC lakes as sites of "monster" or unknown-creature traditions, often with only a few reports per lake:

- **Somenos Lake** – Mentioned as a monster-bearing lake, details scarce.

- **Lake Tagai (Tag)** – A named monster "Tag" reportedly associated with this lake.

- **Seton Lake** – Linked more strongly to giant white sturgeon than to a distinct serpent, but still discussed in cryptid circles.

These lesser-known lakes don't yet have the kind of sighting volume that Ogopogo and Shuswaggi do, but they're worth flagging for anyone building a bigger Canadian water-monster map.

4. VANCOUVER ISLAND & ISLAND LAKE MONSTERS

Most of Vancouver Island's water cryptid lore is coastal (inlets, sounds, and open ocean), but at least one named lake monster shows up in lists:

- **Tsinquaw – Vancouver Island**Some catalogues of Canadian lake monsters list **Tsinquaw** as a Vancouver Island lake entity, though public details are thin. It's usually mentioned alongside Ogopogo and Shuswaggi in "Canadian water monster" round-ups.

Because of the lack of detailed, date-stamped sightings, Tsinquaw remains more of a line item than an active case file — at least in open sources.

5. COASTAL CROSSOVERS (BRIEFLY)

Strictly speaking, these aren't "lake monsters," but if you're building a serious BC water-cryptid reference, you can't ignore:

- **Cadborosaurus ("Caddy") – Coastal inlets & bays**A classic West Coast sea serpent described as a long, serpentine creature with horse- or camel-like head, anterior and posterior flippers, and a series of humps. Over 200 sightings have been collected from British Columbia's coastal waters, especially Cadboro Bay, Saanich Inlet, and nearby channels.

Caddy belongs more to your "sea monster / coastal serpent" section than a strictly lake-based index, but in a BC context, it absolutely sits on the same family tree of water mysteries.

6. USING THIS INDEX IN THE FIELD

As with the Bigfoot appendix, this index isn't meant to be an armchair collection — it's meant to point you toward **live terrain**:

- **Okanagan Lake** — If you're on the water between late August and early October, especially around Rattlesnake Island and the central basin, you're inside prime Ogopogo window.

- **Shuswap Lake** — Long, complex shoreline and multiple arms; Murdoch Point, Salmon Arm, and channels with deep drop-offs are the places where some of the best Shuswaggi cases come from.

- **Skaha / Osoyoos / satellite lakes** — Watch for wave anomalies, sudden organized humps, or anything like a single, smooth wake running against normal patterns, especially in calm conditions.

- **Lesser-known lakes** — Tagai, Somenos, Seton and similar "name-checked" lakes are ideal quiet-season reconnaissance targets if you want to work ahead of the curve.

And, as always, the same rule applies here as it does with Bigfoot:

You don't need a boatload of gear to contribute something meaningful. A phone camera, a notebook, and the discipline to write down **exactly what you saw and when** will put you ahead of 90% of witnesses.

If you're on a lonely dock at dusk, and the lake suddenly goes glass-calm except for one long, rolling wake that isn't attached to a boat or a log — this appendix is just here to remind you:

You're not the first person in BC to see something like that.You almost certainly won't be the last.

APPENDIX C — BC UFO & SKY PHENOMENA RECORDS

A working field index of British Columbia's unexplained aerial events

Note to the reader: This appendix is a **field-use catalogue**, not an encyclopedic government archive. British Columbia has one of the highest rates of UFO reports in Canada, but detailed, location-specific case files are scattered across newsrooms, MUFON logs, Canadian government documents, civilian databases, and thousands of personal accounts that never make it online.

What you'll find here is a **practical, investigator-ready index**: the major cases, clusters, flaps, and repeat-event regions — enough to recognize patterns, mark hotspots on a map, and understand why BC remains one of Canada's UFO epicentres.

This index includes **UFOs, UAPs, anomalous lights, structured craft**, and **mountain-light phenomena** that defy simple explanation.

1. METRO VANCOUVER & THE LOWER MAINLAND

Even in populated regions, the number of "high-strangeness" aerial reports in BC is significant.

Vancouver (General Region) — Consistent Multi-Decade Activity

BC's largest cluster of publicly reported UFO sightings. Includes:

- **Triangular craft over Vancouver (multiple years)**Repeated reports of silent, low-flying triangles with amber or red lights.

- **Fast-moving white or blue spheres over the North Shore mountains**Often described as "ping-pong ball lights" that accelerate instantly.

Vancouver Airport (YVR) Vicinity — Pilots & Controllers

Though many cases remain confidential, aviation-adjacent witnesses frequently report:

- Objects pacing aircraft on approach

- Silent lights above cloud deck

- Odd radar returns later dismissed as "weather"

The mix of mountains, ocean, and aviation traffic creates an extremely "hot" zone for aerial anomalies.

Surrey / Delta / White Rock — Coastal Sky Oddities

High number of:

- Orange orbs

- "Candle flame" lights drifting inland

- Silent, low-altitude disc-shaped lights over Boundary Bay

These are usually seen during calm-weather nights.

2. FRASER VALLEY & MISSION–ABBOTSFORD CORRIDOR

A surprising number of "structured craft" sightings come from this region.

Mission / Hatzic Area

Home to repeated reports of:

- Large triangular craft

- Slow-moving rectangular lights

- Formation-flying orbs

Tree-lined rural roads and wide sky visibility make this a prime observation area.

Abbotsford / Chilliwack

Reports include:

- "Chevron-shaped" craft gliding silently over farmland

- Brilliant white spheres dropping vertically into fields

- Pulsing lights along the mountains near Cultus Lake

3. THE OKANAGAN — A MULTI-PHENOMENA VALLEY

The Okanagan isn't just Ogopogo territory — it's also one of BC's top UFO corridors.

Kelowna / Okanagan Mountain Park

Dozens of cases spanning decades:

- Pulsing orbs rising over the lake

- Silent discs crossing between valley walls

- "Searchlight-like" beams from above cloud level

- Orange spheres hovering then vanishing instantly

Penticton / Naramata Bench

Winery workers and night-shift employees often report:

- Metallic, reflective objects at sunset

- Multi-light craft flying low over vineyards

- High-speed streaks moving north–south along the lake

Vernon / Coldstream

Common reports:

- Small bright spheres

- Red-orange orbs drifting toward Silver Star Mountain

- Formation lights over valley floor

The Okanagan's long north–south orientation creates a natural "sky funnel" — perfect for spotting anomalies.

4. SHUSWAP REGION — UFOs AND LAKE LIGHTS

Already known for lake monsters, Shuswap also produces intriguing aerial reports.

Salmon Arm / Sorrento

- Bright orbs hovering over the lake

- "Headlight-like" beams shining downward from silent objects

- Fast horizontal streaks captured on night-vision camera

Chase / Adams Lake

Remote cabins report:

- Lights emerging from behind mountains

- Objects rising vertically from treeline

- Pulsing orbs drifting long distances

5. VANCOUVER ISLAND — MOUNTAINS, OCEAN, AND STRANGE LIGHTS

The Island is one of BC's most mysterious aerial hotspots — partly because of its isolation, and partly because it has long been associated with supernatural traditions.

Victoria / Saanich Peninsula

Coastal watchers report:

- Disc-like silver objects reflecting sunlight

- Cigar-shaped craft passing over Haro Strait

- Stationary bright spheres hovering offshore

Nanaimo / Ladysmith

Regular sightings include:

- Orange-red orbs rising from the ocean

- Multi-light objects drifting inland

- Blue-white flashes with no thunder

Port Alberni / Tofino / Pacific Rim

Remote coastline = better sky visibility:

- Silent lights moving at high altitude over open ocean

- Large glowing spheres seen "emerging" from the horizon

- Objects performing 90-degree turns — a classic UAP signature

Campbell River / North Island

Increasingly strong reports in the last decade:

- Bright white or yellow orbs over remote logging roads

- Formation lights flying low over forest canopy

- Unexplained vertical ascents — dead straight up

6. HAIDA GWAII — ANCIENT STORIES & MODERN SIGHTINGS

Haida oral tradition includes powerful sky beings and spirit lights. Today, the same region has modern equivalents:

- Slow-moving orange orbs over the ocean

- Flickering white lights above mountaintops

- Brilliant flashes seen from isolated villages

Many reports describe lights that appear **intelligent** in movement — pacing boats, matching direction, or moving reactively.

7. THE GREAT BEAR RAINFOREST & BELLA COOLA

One of the most remote places in Canada — and home to some of its strangest aerial events.

- Large orange spheres drifting down valley systems

- Bright white orbs hovering over inlet waters

- Nocturnal "forest glows" seen through heavy weather

Fishermen regularly report "stars that move where stars shouldn't."

8. THE CARIBOO, PRINCE GEORGE & THE INTERIOR PLATEAU

High open sky, low population, perfect for sky-watching.

Prince George

- Classic glowing orbs

- Fast-moving light streaks

- Multiple-object formations

Williams Lake / Quesnel

- Orange-red lights moving low over lakes

- Structured craft with two or three lights

- "Domed disc" reports (rare but persistent)

9. NORTHWEST BC — NASS, SKEENA & STEWART CORRIDORS

This region blends Bigfoot hotspots, vanishing stories, and bizarre lights.

- Brilliant white orbs along river corridors

- Lights performing "zig-zag" movements

- Multi-witness sightings by truckers and highway crews

Highway 37 is especially known for strange night-sky activity.

10. ROCKY MOUNTAIN TRENCH & EASTERN BC

The mountain trench creates a natural "sky highway."

Revelstoke / Golden / Valemount

- Light formations flying along valley axis

- Objects vanishing into cloud banks

- High-altitude zig-zag movement patterns

11. UFO "FLAPS" — YEARS WITH SPIKES IN ACTIVITY

Across multiple databases, BC shows elevated activity during:

- **1960s** — Disc reports, Cold War era wave

- **1972–1974** — Province-wide increase in multi-light sightings

- **1994–1996** — Repeated orange-orb cases

- **2010–2014** — Dramatic spike in Lower Mainland reports

- **2019–2024** — Rise of cell-phone video submissions; increase in orbs

The patterns almost always coincide with:

1. High pressure, calm evenings

2. Clear sky between mountains

3. Lakes or ocean in close proximity

4. Witnesses outdoors (camping, fishing, hiking)

12. SPECIAL CASES & HIGH-STRANGENESS REPORTS

These are the outliers — the ones that stick with you.

Structured Triangular Craft Over the Fraser Valley

Silent, jet-black, armed with three bright corner lights.Shape consistent with the "international triangle" sightings.

Objects Entering/Exiting Water (Multiple Regions)

Rare, but reported in:

- Okanagan Lake

- Georgia Strait

- West Coast Vancouver Island

These "transmedium" behaviors match global UAP reports.

The Silent Low Flyover

Often described as:

- A massive dark shape

- Too slow for a plane

- Too silent for a helicopter

- Passing directly overhead

The explanation?Unknown — but consistent across BC.

13. WHAT THIS INDEX TELLS US

Across British Columbia, UFO and UAP sightings share several **recurring traits**:

- Silent movement

- Intelligent or responsive flight paths

- Rapid acceleration

- Hovering

- Vertical ascents

- Orange or red glowing spheres

- Triangular craft

- Water adjacency

- Mountain-valley travel corridors

BC's combination of **isolated wilderness**, **deep valleys**, **ocean access**, and **long Indigenous history of sky-beings** makes it one of the most complex aerial-phenomena environments in North America.

14. FIELD NOTES FOR INVESTIGATORS

Whether you're hiking near Tofino, driving the Coquihalla, fishing in the Shuswap, or camping in the Nass, remember:

- Watch the **mountain horizons**

- Look for lights that move **against wind direction**

- Observe whether an object moves with **purpose**

- Note the **shape** of any formation

- Record **time, direction, colour, duration, and behaviour**

- And if you can capture video — hold your phone steady, landscape mode, 10+ seconds minimum

You don't need night-vision or radar to spot something extraordinary.

BC's skies have been strange for **thousands of years** — long before the word "UFO" ever existed.

And they're still strange today.

APPENDIX D — Indigenous Lore & Sky Beings
Ancient Stories of the Lights Above British Columbia

Note: This appendix does *not* attempt to define, reduce, or reinterpret Indigenous teachings. These accounts are broad, respectful summaries gathered from publicly shared stories, cultural education programs, published works, and oral-tradition material already made available by the Nations themselves.

Indigenous sky lore is profoundly deep — far deeper than anything a single appendix could cover. What's presented here is a field-use framework: themes, patterns, and stories that help illuminate how ancient sky traditions overlap with modern "UFO" or "unexplained lights" sightings.

1. The Land Before the Word "UFO" Existed

Long before settlers arrived — long before the idea of "flying saucers" or "extraterrestrials" entered popular culture — the First Peoples of British Columbia already carried rich traditions of **beings from the sky, lights that moved with purpose**, and encounters with **non-human intelligences that dwelled above the mountains**.

These stories were never framed as "aliens."They were **Sky People.Star Beings.Watchers.Messengers.Transformers**.

They were part of the world, not outside of it — beings woven into the cosmology of land, water, sky, animals, ancestors, and spiritual law.

What stands out across BC's cultural landscape is how widespread sky lore is:

- The **Haida**, with their Sky Realms and supernatural beings descending from the upper world

- The **Nłaka'pamux**, with powerful sky visitors

- The **Stó:lō** and **Coast Salish**, with stories of beings arriving on beams of light

- The **Secwépemc** and **Syilx**, with star-beings and sky guardians

- The **Dene**, **Tahltan**, and **Gitxsan**, whose stories describe luminous spirits moving between mountaintops

- The **Kwakwaka'wakw**, with thunderbird traditions that include transformative sky power

- The **Tsimshian** and **Nisga'a**, who describe spirit-lights passing over valleys

These narratives may differ in name and symbolism, but their core theme is consistent:

The sky has always been alive with presence.

2. The Haida: Beings From the Upper World

Haida cosmology is famously sophisticated. Their world is divided into realms:

- **The World Above (Supernatural sky realm)**

- **The Mortal World**

- **The Undersea Realm**

Sky Beings (or "those who move above") appear in stories as:

- **Powerful ancestors**

- **Shape-shifting beings**

- **Messengers**

- **Visitors arriving from the sky realm**

In some accounts, these beings descend on beams of light, or appear in bird-like or luminous form.They interact with humans, test character, bring knowledge, or alter destiny.

Some oral traditions describe:

- **Stars that move with intention**

- **Lights that descend and transform into beings**

- **Visitors who come during times of imbalance**

These are not "craft" or "machines," but **intelligent presences** linked to the sky realm itself.

3. Coast Salish & Stó:lō Stories — Lights, Messengers & Watchers

Among Coast Salish peoples — whose territory spans Vancouver, the Fraser Valley, Gulf Islands, and beyond — sky lore is deeply tied to cycles, omens, and transformations.

Common themes include:

• **Star People / Sky People**

Beings who come from above to guide, warn, or guard.

• **Lights that follow travellers**

Night travellers in the old days reported lights that moved alongside them — not threatening, but watchful.

• Visitors arriving in luminous form

Some stories describe a being descending as a bright light, transforming upon landing.

• Beings who "walk down the sky"

This metaphor appears in several Coast Salish teachings — describing descent, presence, and a boundary-crossing between realms.

These teachings predate modern UFO concepts by centuries.

4. The Nlaka'pamux & Interior Sky Visitors

Interior Salish groups, including the Nlaka'pamux, Secwépemc, and Syilx/Okanagan peoples, have traditions involving:

- **Luminous sky beings**

- **Visitors descending on ridgelines**

- **Star ancestors**

- **Great lights moving along valley corridors**

These stories often describe:

- Bright objects traveling silently

- Lights moving against wind

- Sudden descents over lakes

- Glowing figures on mountaintops

Much of this overlaps with modern reports from the Okanagan, Nicola Valley, Shuswap, and Thompson River regions — places that consistently generate UAP activity today.

5. The Dene, Tahltan & Northern Nations — The Sky as a Highway

Northern sky cultures recognize the night sky as a living, interactive environment.

Common elements:

• Travelling Lights

Lights that move between mountains, often interpreted as ancestors, spirit messengers, or sky-beings traveling their pathways.

• Beings who come from the stars

Some traditions speak of beings who came long ago from the sky realm and taught survival, hunting practices, or spiritual law.

• Lights entering or emerging from the landscape

Certain valleys and mountain gaps are said to be "doorways" where spirits travel between worlds — descriptions surprisingly similar to modern transmedium UAP (air/water/land crossing) reports.

• Lights seen above hunting camps

These stories are old and widespread, often describing luminous orbs drifting silently across the sky, observing from a distance.

6. Gitxsan, Nisga'a & Tsimshian — Valley Lights & Sky Trails

The Skeena, Nass, and coastal mountain regions have abundant lore involving:

- **Spirit lights moving along river corridors**

- **Lights appearing before major life events**

- **Sky guardians watching travelers**

- **Powerful beings that inhabit specific mountains**

These lights weren't feared — they were understood as part of the spiritual fabric of the land.

What's compelling is how often modern truckers, residents, and hunters on Highway 37 describe **the exact same thing**:

Silent lights drifting along the valley, pacing vehicles, changing direction intelligently, or hovering over river confluences.

The continuity across centuries is impossible to miss.

7. Kwakwaka'wakw & Thunderbird Traditions

Thunderbird stories are sometimes mistakenly lumped into "giant bird" mythology, but among the Kwakwaka'wakw they are far more:

- **Sky beings of immense intelligence**

- **Controllers of thunder, lightning, and transformation**

- **Visitors who move between realms**

Their eyes are said to flash lightning.Their wings create thunder.Their presence marks cycles of change.

Some modern witnesses report:

- Enormous dark silhouettes above coastal valleys

- Sudden lightning-like flashes without storms

- Tremendous silent shadows crossing moonlit sky

While these may not be literal Thunderbirds, the echoes of the old stories remain strong in the region's sky phenomena.

8. Mountain Lights — The Old Stories Before "UFOs"

Across many Nations in BC, lights on mountains are described as:

- **Guardians**

- **Ancestral presences**

- **Warning signs**

- **Orbs of intention rather than simple illumination**

Haida, Nuxalk, Coast Salish, Secwépemc, and Interior groups all have versions of:

- Lights drifting along ridges

- Lights hovering

- Lights moving in straight, purposeful lines

- Lights appearing during liminal times — dusk, dawn, storms, or deaths

To an Indigenous worldview, these lights aren't inexplicable.They're part of the world's spiritual architecture.

9. Water, Mountains & Sky: A Connected Cosmology

One striking element across BC's sky lore is that **water beings, land beings, and sky beings overlap.**

In many teachings:

- Sky beings become land beings

- Land beings become water beings

- Water beings become sky beings again

Transformation is normal.

In cryptid or paranormal research, we categorize everything: Bigfoot here, UFOs there, lake monsters over there.

But Indigenous cosmology sees the boundaries as porous — a world of **interwoven realms**, not separate phenomena.

Interestingly, modern reports increasingly reflect that:

- UFOs near Bigfoot hotspots

- Lights over lake-monster waters

- Aerial anomalies above ancient sacred sites

Indigenous knowledge has been describing that interconnectedness for thousands of years.

10. How Investigators Should Approach This Material

If you're researching UFOs or sky phenomena in BC, there are a few guiding principles:

1. Treat sacred stories with respect

They are not "cryptid data."They are living teachings.

2. Recognize that these traditions are older than any modern sighting

They offer context — not "evidence," but *perspective*.

3. Don't try to force Western labels onto Indigenous cosmology

"Sky beings" or "star people" are not the same thing as "aliens," "craft," or "extraterrestrials."

4. Understand that many Nations distinguish between:

- **ancestors**

- **spirits**

- **sky beings**

- **transformative entities**

— categories that don't align neatly with UFO terminology.

5. Listen. Ask permission. Learn place by place.

Every Nation has its own teachings.There is no "universal Indigenous UFO story."

11. A Final Note: The Old Lights Are Still Here

As you travel across British Columbia — whether you're hiking a ridge at dusk, paddling a still inlet, or standing on a lonely forest road — it's worth remembering:

Long before anyone talked about "UFOs,"people here already knew the sky was active.

Lights moved with intention.Beings crossed between realms.Visitors descended when something was out of balance.And the boundary between earth and sky was never fully closed.

Modern sightings aren't a new phenomenon.They're a continuation of something much older —a conversation between the land, the sky, and the people who pay attention.

APPENDIX E — BC MISSING PERSONS & WILDERNESS VANISHINGS DATABASE
A Field Index of British Columbia's Most Puzzling Disappearances

Note to the reader: This database is *not* a complete record of every person missing in British Columbia.

Many families choose privacy.Many cases remain under seal or unresolved in RCMP archives.Many Northern disappearances never made the news.

What this appendix provides is a **working index** of wilderness vanishings, remote-region cases, and high-strangeness disappearances that have shaped the province's reputation as one of the most mysterious and unforgiving landscapes in North America.

This list blends *documented missing-person cases*, *culturally significant mysteries*, and *patterns repeatedly noted by search-and-rescue professionals*.It is intentionally written for researchers, not tabloids.

SECTION 1 — VANCOUVER ISLAND VANISHINGS

Dense rainforest, steep drainages, fast fog, and sudden weather shifts.

1. The Carmanah Valley Disappearances (Multiple Years)

One of the Island's most dangerous regions: deep rainforest, slick ravines, and virtually no cell coverage. Several hikers and solo travelers have vanished here since the 1980s with no trace recovered.

Patterns:

- Zero remains recovered

- Dense canopy blocking aerial searches

- Frequent "wrong sound" reports by SAR teams (silence, sudden stillness)

2. The Strathcona Provincial Park Cases

Vancouver Island's highest mountains and deepest backcountry.

- **Early 1990s–Present** — Multiple solo hikers vanish without equipment recovered.

- SAR teams often comment on the *scale* and *complexity* of the terrain.

Possible contributing factors:

- Glacial tarns

- Snow caves

- Steep bluffs

- Rapid whiteouts

But several disappearances remain inexplicable even with experience behind them.

3. Missing Kayakers & Small-Boaters (West Coast Inlets)

The Pacific Rim coastline regularly produces strange vanishings:

- Kayaks found upright and fully intact

- Personal items still secured

- No sign of the paddler

Some searches report *persistent lights offshore* seen during SAR operations — logged as "unidentified" but never pursued.

SECTION 2 — THE FRASER VALLEY & COQUIHALLA CORRIDOR

Highway disappearances, abrupt vanishings, and steep-walled terrain.

4. The Coquihalla "No-Trace" Cases

Over several decades, RCMP files document hikers or motorists who:

- Pull over on the highway

- Leave their vehicle

- Vanish

In some cases:

- Snowfall was light and fresh

- Tracks simply stop

- Ground-search dogs lose the trail in open terrain

5. Chilliwack Lake Provincial Park

A region with repeated:

- Disappearances

- Missing campers

- Solo hikers who vanish between well-marked trails

Some SAR volunteers report a "pattern of directional confusion" where subjects appear to walk into increasingly dangerous terrain without apparent reason.

SECTION 3 — OKANAGAN & INTERIOR PLATEAU

Where high summer heat meets steep canyons and deep lakes.

6. The Bear Creek / Westside Road Cluster

A series of vanishings near Kelowna's Westside Road between the 1990s and present day. Victims often vanish close to:

- Sheer drop-offs

- Loose scree

- Dense pine stands

However, several cases have no environmental explanation — dogs lose scent immediately.

7. Lake Okanagan "Boat Without Occupant" Cases

Over decades, several boats have been found:

- Engine idling

- Fishing gear still out

- No operator found

Drowning is the official explanation, but the complete absence of remains in such a heavily searched lake is unusual.

8. Nicola Valley / Merritt Area

Multiple disappearances in open ranchland and forested ridges.

Features noted by SAR:

- Sudden ground fog forming in early morning

- Long gaps in trackable boot prints

- Personal items found neatly placed or untouched

SECTION 4 — SHUSWAP & THOMPSON

Rugged country with overlapping Bigfoot and UFO reports.

9. Shuswap Backcountry Vanishings

Several hunters have gone missing in remote arms of Shuswap Lake:

- Camps left intact

- Fire still smouldering

- No signs of struggle

Dog teams commonly lose the trail at rocky outcrops.

10. Adams Lake — The "Silent Campsite" Cases

Campers vanish leaving:

- Organized gear

- Food prepped

- Vehicles locked

No footprints or drag marks lead away.

Local SAR teams privately describe these cases as "some of the hardest we've worked."

SECTION 5 — KOOTENAYS & SOUTHEAST BC

Sheer alpine terrain where lost people rarely reappear.

11. Glacier & Valhalla Provincial Parks

Disappearances here often involve:

- Climbers

- Photographers

- Experienced solo hikers

Consistent features:

- Last GPS ping near a ridge

- Zero recovered remains

- Sudden weather walls cutting off search windows

12. The Slocan / New Denver Mysteries

A region long considered "strange" by locals:

- Lights in the valleys

- Sudden disorientation

- Missing hikers found far off predicted path (in rare recoveries)

Not all vanishings here are benign.

SECTION 6 — NORTHERN BC: NASS, SKEENA & STEWART

Some of the wildest terrain in Canada — barely mapped, rarely searched fully.

13. Nass Valley Disappearances

Several hunters and small groups have vanished here, often without any trace:

- Camps intact

- High-calibre rifles left behind

- Tracks ending abruptly in moss or stone

Search teams often report **unusual lights** during overnight operations.

14. Stewart–Cassiar Highway (Hwy 37) Corridor

Truckers and RCMP note several cases stretching back decades:

- Motorists who vanish between communities

- Vehicles found with full fuel tanks

- No sign of forced entry or wildlife activity

This is also one of BC's highest-strangeness UFO corridors — a rare overlap.

15. Terrace & Kalum Lake Region

Several older cases involve:

- Hunters who walked short distances from camp

- Never seen again

- Only a rifle or pack recovered

Terrain is extremely steep, but lack of remains is unusual.

SECTION 7 — GREAT BEAR RAINFOREST & CENTRAL COAST

Deep fjords, remote villages, and zero margin for error.

16. Bella Coola Valley Vanishings

Reports spanning 50+ years:

- Residents disappearing on short walks

- Loggers vanishing between road segments

- Tourists who step off a trail and are never found

The valley walls climb almost vertically — yet several disappearances lack the expected fall evidence.

17. Ocean Inlets & Small-Boat Mysteries

Throughout the Great Bear Rainforest:

- Boats recovered intact

- Radios still functioning

- Personal floatation devices left behind

No bodies ever recovered.

SECTION 8 — THE FAR NORTH: DEASE LAKE, ATLIN, FORT NELSON REGION

Sparse population, vast wilderness, minimal RCMP coverage.

18. Dease Lake / Cassiar Triangle Cases

A cluster of vanishings over decades:

- Hunters

- Prospectors

- Highway travelers

Often with:

- Camps undisturbed

- Tracks vanishing on hard ground

- Vehicle parked normally on highway shoulder

19. Atlin Plateau Disappearances

Large, treeless plateaus where visibility should be good — yet multiple people have disappeared without trace.

SAR patterns:

- Dogs lose scent abruptly

- Helicopter teams report "nothingness"

- Weather shifts extremely fast

20. Northern Rockies (Muncho / Liard Area)

Well-known to SAR:

- Several hikers vanish near hot springs and lookout routes

- Trails are clear

- Weather benign

- No scavenger signs or clothing found

SECTION 9 — CROSS-REGIONAL PATTERNS

Across the entire province, several patterns emerge:

1. Campsites Found Intact

Fire warm, food out, bedrolls unused — but the person gone.

2. Tracks That End Abruptly

A common anomaly across BC's mountain terrain.

3. Dogs Losing Scent Instantly

Suggesting airborne scent dispersal or severe terrain complexity.

4. Sudden Weather Walls

Fog, rain curtains, low cloud insertion — sometimes unnaturally fast.

5. Disappearances Near Bodies of Water

Especially deep lakes or steep-banked rivers.

6. Overlap With Other Phenomena

Some vanishings occur in:

- Bigfoot hotspot areas

- UFO corridors

- Low-flying light regions

- High electromagnetic disturbance zones

Not proof — but patterns worth documenting.

SECTION 10 — A RESEARCHER'S NOTE

Across hundreds of cases, one truth becomes clear:

**British Columbia is not simply "dangerous."It is complex. Ancient.
Layered. Alive.**

Many vanishings are explainable — exposure, hypothermia, falls,
misadventure.But others defy both logic and experience.

Search-and-rescue personnel will privately tell you:

- Some forests "feel wrong."

- Some trails "shift."

- Some valleys go *too quiet*.

- Some disappearances make no operational sense.

If you walk into these landscapes, do it with respect, preparation, and an
understanding that **humans are not the apex in BC's deeper
wilderness**.

APPENDIX F — THE CROSSroads MAP
Where Bigfoot, UFOs, Lake Monsters & Vanishings Overlap in British Columbia

A Note to the Reader:

The following "map" is not a graphic — it's a **researcher's map**, built from patterns, clusters, and long-running observations across British Columbia's wilderness.

These overlaps do *not* imply a single cause.They simply show that certain landscapes produce **multiple types of unexplained phenomena**, often far more frequently than surrounding regions.

The deeper you study BC, the more you learn a simple truth:**Some valleys aren't just remote — they're active.**

1. Why Overlaps Matter

After cataloguing hundreds of sightings, vanishings, and aerial anomalies, something becomes unmistakable:

Certain regions show repeated contact points between categories.

- Bigfoot sightings + UFO reports

- Lake-monster sightings + missing paddlers

- Vanishings in areas with intense night-sky activity

- Remote valleys with both creature encounters and anomalous light patterns

At first, you think it's coincidence.Then the pattern repeats.And repeats again.

BC is large — 944,000 square kilometres.Random overlap shouldn't show clear clusters.

But it does.

This appendix identifies the **ten biggest convergence zones** in the province.

2. THE TOP CONVERGENCE ZONES OF BRITISH COLUMBIA

Below are the regions where **multiple mystery types** overlap consistently.

For each zone, you'll find:

- **Primary mysteries present**

- **What the land is like**

- **Why it may produce anomalies**

- **Field notes for researchers**

ZONE 1 — HARRISON LAKE & THE CHEHALIS CORRIDOR

Bigfoot • UFOs • Vanishings • Ancient Lore

This is *the* crossroads of British Columbia.

What overlaps here:

- Highest concentration of Sasquatch sightings in Canada

- Recurring UFO reports along valley walls

- Hikers disappearing from short trails

- Stó:lō sky-being and "wildman" traditions

- Strange nocturnal lights over Chehalis peaks

Terrain: Sheer mountain spines, deep fjord-like lake arms, impenetrable forest.

Field note: Night watchers often report *silent orange or white orbs* drifting low along the lake — almost skimming the water.

ZONE 2 — OKANAGAN LAKE (KELOWNA TO NARAMATA)

Ogopogo • UFOs • Bigfoot (peripheral) • Missing boaters

The Okanagan Valley is built like a natural runway — a straight corridor of water and mountains.

What overlaps here:

- Ogopogo sightings (120+ years of reports)

- Several "boat without occupant" cases

- Pulsing orbs and craft-like lights seen from both shores

- Bigfoot sightings near Trepanier, Bear Creek, and Westside Road

- Interior Salish sky lore

Terrain: Long deep lake, fast weather shifts, thermal currents, cliff-lined sections.

Field note:UFO reports peak during the same months Ogopogo traditionally appears (late summer to early fall).

ZONE 3 — SHUSWAP LAKE & ADAMS LAKE SYSTEM

Shuswaggi • UFOs • Bigfoot • Vanishings

What overlaps here:

- Shuswaggi lake-monster sightings

- Angler-recorded anomalous wakes (2019, 2023)

- Bigfoot sightings in surrounding arms and draws

- Hunters vanishing near Adams Lake

- Persistent light phenomena over the lake at night

Terrain: Complex shoreline, multiple lake arms, ridge-to-ridge funnels.

Field note: Local SAR teams privately acknowledge "unusual sky lights" seen during several searches.

ZONE 4 — FRASER CANYON (HOPE → LYTTON → SPENCES BRIDGE)

Bigfoot • UFOs • Highway vanishings • Indigenous sky lore

What overlaps here:

- Multiple historical Sasquatch sightings

- Triangular craft reported above canyon walls

- Travelers vanishing along side roads and pullouts

- Nlaka'pamux teachings involving sky visitors

Terrain: Vertical walls, narrow sky view, deep acoustics.

Field note: Truckers frequently report "stars that move wrong."

ZONE 5 — VANCOUVER ISLAND WEST COAST (TOFINO → UCLUELET → KYUQUOT)

UFOs • Maritime vanishings • Bigfoot (inland) • Ocean anomalies

What overlaps here:

- Coastal UFO flaps (multiple decades)

- Kayakers disappearing with boats found intact

- Bigfoot activity in inland valleys (Nahmint, Kennedy, Clayoquot)

- Spirit-light stories from Nuu-chah-nulth culture

Terrain: Rugged coast, storm belts, sudden fog walls.

Field note: Pilots on coastal routes have repeatedly reported silent "pearlescent lights" pacing their aircraft.

ZONE 6 — BELLA COOLA & THE GREAT BEAR RAINFOREST

Bigfoot • UFOs • Vanishings • Spirit-light traditions

What overlaps here:

- Sasquatch encounters in river corridors

- Vanishings in short travel distances

- Large luminous orbs moving down valley systems

- Nuxalk stories of sky beings descending

Terrain: Almost vertical valley walls, rainforest canopy, long fjords.

Field note: Fishermen have reported lights rising **from below the tree line**, not above it.

ZONE 7 — NASS VALLEY & NORTHWEST CORRIDOR (TERRACE → KITWANGA → MEZIADIN)

UFOs • Bigfoot • Vanishings • Highway anomalies

What overlaps here:

- Bigfoot hotspots along river systems

- UFOs pacing vehicles on Hwy 37

- Silent lights above the volcanics

- Hunters disappearing without trace

Terrain: Basalt plateaus, volcanic fields, mist-laden valleys.

Field note: One of the few places where **all four categories** overlap strongly.

ZONE 8 — HAIDA GWAII

Sky beings • UFOs • Luminous phenomena • Ocean anomalies

What overlaps here:

- Haida accounts of sky visitors and descending lights

- Modern reports of orange orbs over the ocean

- Unknown objects entering/exiting the sea

- Ancient stories of beings arriving from the upper world

Terrain: Remote archipelago, open ocean, massive sky visibility.

Field note: Local mariners describe the lights as "too low to be stars and too steady to be aircraft."

ZONE 9 — KOOTENAYS (NELSON → AINSWORTH → KASLO)

Bigfoot • UFOs • Vanishings • Mountain-lights

What overlaps here:

- Road-crossing Sasquatch sightings

- Hikers vanishing near ridgelines

- Repeated canyon-light sightings over Kootenay Lake

- Thunderbird and sky-spirit traditions in some regional Nations

Terrain: Glacial lakes, scree cliffs, narrow alpine passes.

Field note: Some locals refer to specific mountaintops as "the watchers."

ZONE 10 — THE STEWART–CASSIAR HIGHWAY (DEASE → ISKUT → STEWART)

UFO corridor • Bigfoot • Remote vanishings • High-strangeness

What overlaps here:

- Some of BC's most credible modern road sightings

- Bigfoot reports in river flats and cutlines

- Motorists vanishing between distant communities

- Bright orbs pacing vehicles

Terrain: Nearly 800 km of wild, sparsely populated highway.

Field note: This is one of the rare places where Bigfoot, UFOs, and vanishings occur *within the same highway segments*.

3. PATTERNS FOUND ACROSS ALL 10 ZONES

Pattern 1: Bodies of water are involved in almost every zone.

- Long lakes

- Fjords

- Ocean channels

- Deep glacial depressions

Water amplifies almost every category: lights, creatures, vanishings.

Pattern 2: Valleys with restricted sky views produce the most UFO reports.

Like long rifle barrels, they funnel movement — or at least the perception of it.

Pattern 3: Bigfoot hotspots and missing-person clusters often overlap.

Not in a supernatural way — but in a *geographical* one.

Areas good for a large animal to hide are also areas where humans can vanisheasily.

Pattern 4: Ancient Indigenous sky lore is strongest in the same zones modern UFO reports cluster.

A meaningful continuity worth deep respect.

Pattern 5: Steep terrain = abrupt scent loss.

SAR teams note that many disappearances occur where scent disperses vertically almost instantly.

Pattern 6: Lakes with monster legends often have documented strange lights above them.

Okanagan Lake and Shuswap are prime examples.

4. FIELD NOTES — USING THE CROSSROADS MAP

If you're planning BC field research, this appendix gives you a blueprint:

- **Pick a crossroads zone** (Zones 1, 2, 3, and 7 are the most active).

- Identify **water + mountains + remote access**.

- Conduct **night watches** near ridge funnels.

- Walk **logging roads at dawn** — the prime time for trackfinds.

- Use **thermal, audio, and skywatch** gear together.

This appendix exists for one purpose:

To help you see where the mysteries stack on top of each other.

In BC, the strangest stories don't live in isolation — they live in clusters.

And once you learn where those clusters are, you never look at the map the same way again.

APPENDIX G: Best place in British Columbia to search for Bigfoot

If your goal is **the single best place in British Columbia to search for Bigfoot**, based on every pattern we've mapped, every historic case file, Indigenous stories, modern reports, SAR anomalies, and overlapping phenomena…

There is **one region** that stands far above the rest.

And that region is:

HARRISON LAKE & THE CHEHALIS CORRIDOR

(The #1 Bigfoot Hotspot in British Columbia — and arguably in Canada)

Let me break it down clearly and practically.

WHY HARRISON IS THE HOTTEST SPOT

1. Longest, Densest History of Sasquatch Reports in Canada

This is where:

- J.W. Burns recorded early "Sasquatch" interviews

- Stó:lō Nation oral histories clearly describe "Sasq'ets"

- Settler reports from the 1800s mention giant, hair-covered beings

- Sightings continue **every decade** to the present

It's the most **consistent** hotspot on record.

2. The Geography Is Perfect for a Large, Intelligent Animal

Harrison Lake area has:

- Steep mountains

- Endless unroaded valleys

- Dark, wet old-growth forest

- Massive berry crops

- Salmon-bearing rivers

- Side valleys almost impossible for humans to access

It is *ideal* habitat for something trying to remain unseen.

3. Modern Encounters Are Still Frequent

Even today, you get:

- Road crossings on forest service roads

- Vocalization reports

- Ridge-line silhouettes

- Rock throwing

- Footprints

- "Pacing in the bush" stories

- Boaters seeing figures on remote shoreline

Local groups quietly treat this as **active territory**.

4. It Sits Directly Between Coastal & Interior Ecosystems

This gives Bigfoot:

- Migration corridors

- Food diversity

- Escape routes

- True deep wilderness

It's a *bridge* habitat that allows movement across half the province.

5. It Overlaps With Other Phenomena

This doesn't prove anything — but it matters for patterns.

Harrison has:

- High UFO report rates

- Strange nocturnal lights

- Unusual sound phenomena

- Missing-person cases in the mountains

Every major BC mystery **crosses paths** here.

WHERE EXACTLY TO GO (Field Research Locations)

Here are the **specific hotspots** within the Harrison region, the places seasoned BC researchers treat as prime ground:

1. North End of Harrison Lake

Remote logging roads with almost no traffic.

2. Chehalis River Valley / Morris Valley Road

Historic Indigenous Sasquatch territory.

3. Sasquatch Provincial Park / Hick's Lake / Deer Lake

Classic sighting zone with good acoustics.

4. Hemlock Valley & Mystery Creek

Known for vocals and night disturbances.

5. Harrison East FSR (Forest Service Road)

Road crossings & deep side drainage activity.

6. Silver River & Big Silver Creek

Prime valley habitat — hard to access.

7. Grizzly Ridge & Bear Mountain area

Rugged, remote, lots of berry crops.

If you wanted one target area for your first expedition:

Harrison East FSR → Big Silver Creek → North Harrison

That corridor has the most recurring pattern of activity in the last 20 years.

THE SECOND-HOTTEST REGION (if you want options)

SHUSWAP LAKE → ADAMS LAKE → TWIN LAKES CORRIDOR

This is a strong #2 because:

- Bigfoot

- Lake monster

- UFOs

- Vanishings

- Deep valleys with few access points

Perfect mixed-phenomena region.

THE THIRD-HOTTEST REGION

BELLA COOLA → GREAT BEAR RAINFOREST

If you want **raw, untouched wilderness** with strong Bigfoot reports and terrifying valley acoustics — this is where to go.

It's harder to reach, but arguably some of the wildest land in North America.

BUT IF YOU ONLY CHOOSE ONE?

If your goal is **maximum chance of a real encounter**, not just scenic terrain:

Go to Harrison.

There's a reason it's the birthplace of the modern word "Sasquatch."

APPENDIX H: The single best place in British Columbia to witness UFOs, strange lights, or unexplained aerial phenomena

If your goal is **the single best place in British Columbia to witness UFOs, strange lights, or unexplained aerial phenomena**, the data from decades of reports, pilot sightings, Indigenous sky lore, SAR accounts, and modern photos all point to **one region** that stands clearly above the rest:

THE OKANAGAN VALLEY — Kelowna to Naramata

(The #1 UFO / UAP / Sky-Light Hotspot in British Columbia)

This isn't just "active."It's **consistently active**, with the strongest combination of:

- Multi-witness sightings

- Repeating patterns

- High daylight and nocturnal UFO activity

- Orb lights

- Craft-like formations

- Transmedium phenomena (objects entering/exiting water)

- Historical Indigenous sky lore

- Pilot and aviation-adjacent reports

- Visible sky corridors between mountain ridges

If Bigfoot's "home base" is Harrison,**UFOs own the Okanagan.**

Let me break this down.

WHY THE OKANAGAN IS #1 FOR UFOs & STRANGE SKY LIGHTS

1. The Valley is a Natural Sky Funnel

The long north–south layout is perfect for:

- Orb movement

- Straight-line trajectories

- Valley-following craft

- Ridge-hovering lights

Witnesses often describe lights *pacing* the valley.

2. Okanagan Lake Has a History of "Lights Rising From Water"

This is one of the rare BC places where people report:

- Lights coming **out** of the lake

- Lights diving **into** the water

- Hovering orbs that drift along the shoreline

These match global UAP "transmedium" patterns.

3. Multi-Generational Witnesses

Residents who've lived in the valley 50+ years often say:

"The lights have always been here."

Reports stretch from the 1960s to 2025.

4. High Volume of Sightings (Even by Canadian Standards)

Year after year, the Okanagan ranks near the top of Canada's UFO regions.

5. Night Sky Visibility is Perfect

Dry climate + warm nights + minimal cloud in summer =prime conditions for sky anomalies.

THE EXACT HOTSPOTS WITHIN THE OKANAGAN

#1. Okanagan Mountain Park (Kelowna side)

This is THE peak UFO-viewing location.

People report:

- Bright orbs gliding above the lake

- Hovering multi-light craft

- Silent "lantern-like" objects sitting above the ridge

- Zig-zag movement patterns

Campers and boaters see these the most.

#2. Naramata Bench / Penticton Ridgebacks

A massive UFO concentration area.

Night-shift workers at wineries and farms often report:

- Metallic daytime discs

- Formation lights

- Orbs drifting down the valley walls

The vast open sky makes everything more visible.

#3. Knox Mountain / Kelowna Foreshore

Urban lights don't kill the sightings here.

Residents frequently see:

- Large orange orbs

- Sudden "star drop" movements

- Lights hovering stationary

- Bright white spheres moving over lake directionally

Often filmed from downtown condos.

#4. Vernon / Coldstream & Silver Star Corridor

This stretch gets:

- Fast-moving "ping-pong ball lights"

- Blue-white streaks

- Red orbs drifting slowly above treeline

One of the province's most underrated UFO zones.

#5. Skaha Lake & Okanagan Falls

A known UFO–Ogopogo overlap zone.

People see:

- Rod-like or cigar-shaped craft

- Long, glowing streaks

- Objects following the lake axis

This region gets a lot of sunrise/sunset sightings.

THE SECOND-BEST UFO REGION IN BC: THE FRASER VALLEY

Mission → Hatzic → Abbotsford

- Triangular craft

- Chevron-shaped objects

- Silent low-altitude passes

- Multiple-witness orb sightings

The valley funnels craft visually the same way the Okanagan does.

THE THIRD-BEST REGION: VANCOUVER ISLAND WEST COAST

Tofino → Ucluelet → Kyuquot

The sky over the open Pacific produces:

- Massive bright orbs on the horizon

- Silent lights pacing small aircraft

- Vertical ascents

- Lights entering the ocean

This is the place to go if you want **coastal UAPs**.

BUT IF YOU WANT THE BEST SHOT AT SEEING SOMETHING?

If you asked every serious UFO researcher in BC one question:

"Where do I go if I want to see something with my own eyes?"

They would almost all say:

"Go to Okanagan Mountain Park after dusk."

Next best:

"Watch the sky from Naramata Bench on a calm, warm night."

APPENDIX I: Single most haunted place in BC

British Columbia has many haunted regions, but if the question is: **"What is the single most haunted place in BC?"**

the answer — based on intensity, consistency, history, and the *sheer density* of reported encounters — is absolutely clear:

THE CARIBOO GOLD RUSH CORRIDOR

(Barkerville → Wells → Quesnel Lake → Likely → Cariboo Mountains)

The most haunted region in British Columbia.

Not just a haunted *building*, or a haunted *town*. A haunted **landscape** — miles of it.

This region is where BC's frontier violence, sudden deaths, gold fever, Indigenous displacement, murder, mining accidents, and remote wilderness all collide. It has **everything** a hotspot needs:

- tragic history

- boomtown chaos

- lost miners

- mass graves

- forest spirits

- ghost towns

- drowned settlements

- abandoned mine shafts

- old hotels

- nighttime apparitions

- ghost lights in the woods

Let's break this down clearly.

WHY THE CARIBOO IS THE MOST HAUNTED REGION IN BC

1. Barkerville — The Most Haunted Town in Western Canada

If you go anywhere in BC for ghosts, go here.

People report:

- children running in the streets at night

- shadow figures in abandoned cabins

- voices behind locked doors

- footsteps on empty boardwalks

- full apparitions inside the old theatre and saloon

Staff, volunteers, and historians *all* have stories.

This isn't lore — this is lived experience.

2. The Cariboo Goldfields Were Violent, Chaotic & Deadly

Tens of thousands of miners came through from 1860–1900.

Hundreds died from:

- mine collapses

- drowning

- sickness

- shootings

- freezing to death on trails

- robbery and murder

Most were buried in unmarked graves or left where they fell.

Haunting is practically baked into the soil.

3. Wells — A Living Ghost Town

The arts community of Wells sits just outside Barkerville, but it has its own long list of paranormal reports:

- figures walking the upper hallways of the Wells Hotel

- doors closing on their own in old miner housing

- music heard in buildings long abandoned

- glowing figures seen on the ridge at night

Local residents consider this normal.

4. Quesnel Lake & Likely — Deep-Water & Backroad Hauntings

This area has some of the eeriest wilderness hauntings in BC:

- ghost lights on backroads

- phantom voices calling from the woods

- pale figures seen near the shoreline

- drowned miners said to appear near the old steamship wrecks

Quesnel Lake is one of the deepest lakes in the world — full of old logging and mining tragedies.

5. The Cariboo/Wells Grey Mountains — The "Silent Forest"

This stretch of mountain wilderness is infamous among hunters and SAR teams for:

- sudden eerie silence

- "being watched" sensations

- disembodied footsteps following trails

- flickering white lights drifting through the trees

- figures seen between trees, then gone

Local Indigenous stories describe forest spirits, shadow beings, and land guardians — all still spoken of today.

THE RUNNER-UP: VANCOUVER ISLAND — The "Ghost Coast"

If BC had a second most haunted region, it's here:

- **Victoria** — The most haunted city in Western Canada

- **Craigdarroch Castle** — full-body apparitions

- **Old Coal Mining Towns** (Cumberland, Nanaimo)

- **West Coast Logging Camps** — ghost loggers & phantom lights

- **Tofino/Ucluelet** — spectral lights, ocean apparitions

But the hauntings are *spread out*.

The Cariboo is concentrated.

THE MOST HAUNTED SPECIFIC LOCATION IN BC

If you want the *single* most haunted **building**, it's:

The Wells Hotel (Wells, BC)

- full apparitions

- footsteps

- room disturbances

- voices

- shadow figures

- repeating hauntings for decades

Followed closely by:

Craigdarroch Castle (Victoria)

But again — buildings are one thing.

THE MOST HAUNTED WILDERNESS AREA

If you want wilderness-only hauntings:

The Great Bear Rainforest (Bella Coola)

Especially:

- Tweedsmuir Park

- Atnarko Corridor

- Hill beside the Bella Coola River

This region blends:

- spirit lights

- glowing figures

- ghost voices

- shapeshifter legends

- strange humanoid sightings at night

But the Cariboo still wins in overall density and documented variety.

SO WHAT IS THE MOST HAUNTED PLACE IN BC?

THE CARIBOO GOLD RUSH CORRIDOR

Barkerville → Wells → Quesnel Lake → Likely → Cariboo Mountains

If you told any professional ghost investigator, historian, or paranormal filmmaker:

"I can only visit one haunted region in BC,"

They would send you here.

From the Author

Thank you for exploring these mysteries with me. British Columbia is a place where the wilderness still holds its secrets, and every trip into the backcountry reminds me how much we still don't understand. My hope is that these stories inspire curiosity, respect for the land, and a sense of wonder for the world just beyond the treeline.

Stay safe out there — and keep listening.